S   HAMS

WOODWARD

ACKNOWLEDGEMENTS ...

This book is published independently but Mervyn Woodward and the publishers wish to thank Lesley Whittaker, Manager of the South Hams Environment Trust, for her help in compiling the Guide and Environment sections in this book.

Whilst extreme care has been taken in compiling this guide, neither the author or publishers accept any liability for errors or mistakes contained within

Woody's Guide
TO THE
SOUTH HAMS
compiled by MERVYN WOODWARD

© Orchard Publications 1995.

ISBN. 1 898964 17 3

Published by
ORCHARD PUBLICATIONS
2 Orchard Close, Chudleigh, Newton Abbot, Devon. TQ13 0LR
Telephone: (01626) 852714

Photography by SCOTT MORRISH
and South Hams Tourist Board page nos. 26, 30 (castle), 81 & 104.

Designed, Typeset and Printed by: SWIFT PRINT, DAWLISH, S. DEVON.

INDEX

FOREWORD

For more than twenty-five years I have enjoyed the privilege of writing for some of the most prestigious and respected guides in the U.K. I have met and written about top chefs and hoteliers, restaurateurs and innkeepers, and have come to appreciate all that goes into the excellence of service and produce that distinguish the very best from the others. The importance of hygiene and proper 'food management' has been a prime consideration in selecting the establishments invited to be in Woody's guide. This, the use of fresh Devon produce wherever possible, the ambience, facilities, atmosphere and welcome are the criteria for being featured in the guide. These standards apply to all the superb hotels, inns and restaurants featured. Similar standards, with the emphasis on value for money and quality apply to the varied attractions and entertainments of other businesses which go to make up the guide. In this, the first Woody's guide, you should find what you are looking for whether you are a resident or a visitor. The guide is about the South Hams, a place of country lanes and wildflowers, high hedges and great expanses of sky - perhaps the nearest thing you will get to Heaven on Earth!

If you can't find what you want here - you must be tired of life.

'Woody'

SOUTH HAMS FOOD & DRINK ASSOCIATION

Lee Mill, Ivybridge, Devon. PL21 9PE
Tel: Plymouth (01752) 895151 Fax: (01752) 691189

The South Hams Food and Drink Association was created to promote the variety and excellence of food and drink produced and served in this unique part of the country.

It is the temperate climate and geographical diversity of the South Hams, ranging from the fringes of Dartmoor, through lush valleys to our beautiful coast, that lends itself so well to the production of the very best food and drink; moorland venison, organic vegetables, out-standing pies and sausages, fresh pasta, biscuits and confectionery, flavoured oils and dressings, cheeses, wine, soft fruits, ice cream, local meats, beer, cider, smoked meats and fish, preserves, wet fish and shell fish, to name but a few.

When you buy produce or eat out at any of our South Hams Food and Drink Association members you can rely on our seal of excellence, safe in the knowledge that not only are you buying quality produce, but also supporting our flourishing food and drink Industry.

To find the best local food and drink look out for our logo, and for a complete list of all our members, up and coming events, ideas for outings, special offers etc contact Natasha Bradley on (01752) 895151.

INTRODUCTION

If you mention the South Hams to people who are strangers to the county you find that many have not heard of this particular area - perhaps this is partly the secret of its timeless magic and individuality, even the name itself is the subject of controversy - Hamms or Hamme is the old English word for low lying meadow or enclosed pasture, and in olden days usually owned by royalty.

Not so long ago, 'The South Hams' indicated a much smaller area than it does now. A highly-favoured triangle with water on two sides, it stretched from the River Erme in the West, to the River Dart in the East, stopping at the level of Modbury and Blackawton to the North. Geographically, this area has certain distinctive features, particularly a very mild climate. Later extensions of the 'South Hams' moved the border northwards to Totnes, and eventually to the main road through south Devon, the A38, while the western boundary moved to the River Yealm.

Now, what we call the 'South Hams' has become the area which the District Council of that name administers. This stretches from the River Tamar in the West, round the outskirts of Plymouth, up onto Dartmoor, and round the back of Torbay to Marldon.

Clearly, such a span has no uniform landscape or environmental theme. except one; that it is one of the loveliest areas of the United Kingdom, and the more interesting for the variety of habitat and architecture it now embraces.

There are four main types of landscape in the South Hams. The Dartmoor wilderness looms on the northern horizon, with the high points above South Brent and Ivybridge forming the rolling, open boundary. The southern extreme is the largely treeless but rich humpback land behind the coast at Bolt head. In between lies the patchwork of agricultural land, with tree-lined rivers, deep valleys and frquent hamlets and villages, while around it sweeps the magnificent coastline, battered by an energetic sea.

The SOUTH HAMS
ENVIRONMENT

The environment of the South Hams is recognised as special by many authorities, and each has implemented protective measures. They range from government level to the most local of all, the Parish. A designation as a Site of Special Scientific Interest (or 'Triple S.I.') lists the flora, fauna or other features which have led to this classification. It is not as effective a means of protection as perhaps it should be, but operates to draw attention to matters which ought to be taken into account. The magnificent coastline is designated 'Heritage Coast', and a good example of the co-operative nature of the work to conserve it is the appointment of a Heritage Coast Officer in this area, jointly by the District Council, Devon County Council and the Countryside Commission. The local 'Green Tourism Initiative' is another joint venture.

Large parts of the South Hams are either designated an 'Area of Outstanding Natural Beauty', or fall within the protective boundaries of the Dartmoor National Park. The District Council imposes town planning limitations by declaring Conservation Areas in towns and villages to protect groupings of buildings, many of which may not be of particular value on their own, but are vital to the character of the heart of a village. The Department of National Heritage is responsible for listing individual buildings as 'of architectural or historical interest.' These are not all grand mansions like the mediaeval magnificence of Dartington Hall, but can be tiny cottages which show the development of domestic living arrangements through the centuries, ruined castles, traditional farmyards, or even fortifications dating from the last War. There are Tree Preservation Orders, which are watched over by the Parish Tree Wardens, who look after newly planted trees, as well as the older specimens which are important in the landscape. The District Council declares Local Nature Reserves, such as that which covers the Kingsbridge and Salcombe estuary, another outstanding natural habitat, which, because it is subject to intense pressure from human activity, requires particularly determined but sensitive management.

The District Council runs a lively Environment Service, which promotes many initiatives within the area. It has a programme of aptly named 'Jigsaw' environmental events throughout the year. They range from story-telling walks through local woods, to guided walks examining local history, wildlife, or geographical features, led by experts, and all well worth attending. They are detailed in leaflets which tell you where to be, how to dress, and how long it will take. These leaflets, together with a wide variety of others which list local beaches, places of interest, town trails, and walks, are available (some of them free) from the Tourist Information Centres in most towns and villages, or the local post office, and some hotels and visitor attractions.

The Orchard Programme promoted by the Environment Service has been a great success, resulting in the establishment of a nursery dedicated to reviving the old apple varieties. South Hams cider was once famous, and commanded a premium price up-country. The orchards had mainly fallen into neglect, thus removing a distinctive feature of the landscape. Grafts from the remaining trees have led to a renewal of availability for re-stocking and you will see newly planted orchard trees as you travel the region, rejoicing in the wonderful old names, such as 'Slack-ma-girdle', 'Dolls Eyes' and 'Greasy Butcher'.

The South Hams Environment Trust is a recently established local charity which helps individuals, councils and other organisations, with environmental work. It draws its funds from the area, and is establishing a group of 'Friends' who support its work to promote the enjoyment and understanding of the countryside, and the preservation of the environment of this very special place. The Trust was closely involved in the campaign to buy the island at South Brent by public subscription. If you wander down the lane below the ancient Church of St. Petroc (call in later, to admire this splendid and historic building) you will be able to enjoy the result. A river island in the Avon, the land bordered by a sixteenth century mill leat, which the local people can now freely enjoy.

Here we have a meadow which has never been subjected to modern farming methods. The initial species count of flowers and plants showed some 120 different kinds; a bird watch on one April day yielded 27 species; and insects, spiders, lichens, and small mammals are all being surveyed on a regular basis, by experts and the local school children. Salmon have been photographed leaping the weir, and shadowy trout can be seen from the bridge, probably it is this which attracts the heron to these waters. Otters used to frequent the place, but no recent trace has been found. The Island is being managed by a local group to preserve it as a wildlife area, and also for quiet enjoyment by its human visitors. It is in some ways unremarkable, with no unduly rare species. Yet that in itself makes it remarkable, as a survival of the rich, wide-ranging mixture of plants, animals, birds and insects which was taken for granted not so very long ago, and which we now have to work hard to restore. You will find fallen trees left to rot, providing habitat for fungi and insects, and thus food for the birds. You will find leaf and twig debris, under which over-wintering hedgehogs can take shelter. You will find long grass, left so that some species can seed, and other areas grazed, so that flowers, herbs and grasses can flourish, without being overwhelmed by tree saplings and brambles. Nettles and brambles also have their place, and you will see them growing on the Island, offering food to butterflies and birds. Other trees with hollow branches offer nesting and feeding room to yet other species, including bats, for whom Devon provides a home for most British species.

The trees of the South Hams are some of the most distinctive features of its landscape. The clumps of Scots Pines on the high points, the dense woods of the valleys, the stunted and twisted isolated thorn trees of Dartmoor's open sweeps, each brings its own richness to the picture. Perhaps the most significant trees for the area are the ones which a casual glance would hardly allow to be described as trees at all, those of the hedgerow. Years ago, farmers managed their hedges as living barriers to confine their stock to their fields, to provide shelter from rain and sun, and browsing to enrich the animals' diets. Some trees were allowed to grow to full height to provide shelter. Every 15 years or so, the hedge was 'layered', 'laid' or 'steeped', and the larger branches were taken for firewood. The others were part severed, laid over, and woven and pegged, to renew the stock-proof barrier. The characteristic South Hams patchwork of rolling fields is due to the survival of hedges here, which have long since been grubbed out in other regions. The government paid grants for this work, and the environmental implications were only realised later. Fields were joined into larger units to make it easier to use more powerful tractors and bigger items of equipment. The huge round bales of hay and silage we see so frequently today illustrate this leap into a bigger scale, when compared with the rectangular bales they are replacing. Of course, there is a whole change in the system of planting, growing, harvesting, storage and animal feeding involved in such a move.

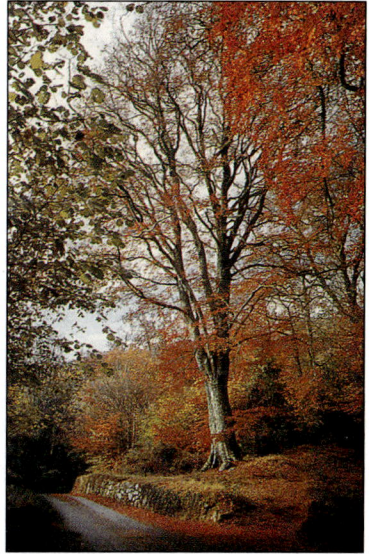

There was a time when farmers were very environmentally unfriendly, but they realised more quickly than many other people what the implications of the changes in agricultural methods were. Things began to get out of balance. Robbed of the thirsty trees around their borders, fields were left with standing water after any prolonged period of rain. Floods followed and created havoc, just as they have on a massively larger scale on the plains of Bangladesh and India, where cutting the trees has caused enormous loss of life over the years, as well as washing away the precious topsoil. All too often heavy rain will bring gushing brown torrents under field gates, taking away the soil and with it, the newly sown crop. The damage is both short and long-term as well as having immediate economic implications in the cost of re-sowing. The wet surface cannot be worked by heavy equipment without compacting it, causing damage to the soil structure by knocking out the air which the soil needs to stay alive. When the soil dries, without the hedges acting as wind-breaks, the soil blows away.

Hedges offer habitat to insects and birds which control pests, and pollinate crops. When they have gone, other methods of control have to be found. Hedges also offer what are now recognised as vital wildlife corridors, allowing populations to move around the countryside to find new mates, new food sources, and room to expand. Much effort now goes into creating these corridors, and the farmers are at the forefront of doing this. They leave wider headlands as they plough, leave some areas uncut, and generally are more aware of the implications of what they do.

As part of this changed mood, the value of a 'proper' hedge is now being recognised. Woodburning stoves need fuel, stock still needs to be confined within the boundaries of the farm, and to be shelted from sun and rain. Hazel trees, commonly found in hedgerows, provide nuts for humans, birds and small mammals, including the attractive (but now rare) dormouse. Hollow trees offer roosting and nesting sites to owls, bats, woodpeckers, and wild bees, hornets and wasps.

Hedgerow management is being promoted in the South Hams area as part of a country-wide pilot study which includes work on how best to deal with the results of flail cutting of hedges. This method of trimming has been adopted by farmers in recent years as a result of a number of factors, not least the loss of the skills of hedge laying. Time presses upon the much smaller work forces on farms today, and the farmer treats his tractor as a sort of combined overcoat and third hand. All in all, it is easier and more efficient to attach a flail cutter to the tractor and drive alongside the hedge. Although the attractions are obvious and understandable, repeated flailing results in a wide, open growth of hedge which animals can break through easily. It is less attractive visually, and less useful to wildlife. The temptation comes to grub it out and replace it with a good fence.

Management plans are evolving which it is hoped will help to generate these hedges as useful wildlife habitat and food sources, while allowing the farmer to retain the ease of trimming. The timing of this procedure is vitally important. Disturbing nesting birds, or stripping away the nuts and berries of their autumn larders is disastrous. Care in planning the cutting programme helps considerably to improve the usefulness of the hedge. Incidentally, should you notice a strip of brightly coloured plastic fluttering incongruously in a hedge, look carefully before you decide it is litter, and should be removed. Young trees are being flagged in this way as a signal to the tractor driver to lift the cutters so that the tree can grow. Then we shall enjoy again the sight of fine specimen trees rising from the field boundaries, a delight to the eye, as well as good shelter for stock and habitat for other creatures.

There is a rule of thumb for estimating the age of a hedge. Count the number of different trees in a 10 metre length, then multiply by 5 to get the age in centuries.

To any reader interested in our hedgerows and wildlife we recommend another of our titles 'The Living History of our Hedgerows'. The author Lesley Chapman, details the envolement of our hedgerows and shows the reader how to date them with some accuracy and define the plantlife within.

There are still remnants of the ancient native oak forests to be found in the South Hams. These complex habitats have been established over hundreds of years, and are to be found in the river valleys of the Yealm, Dart and Avon, with some in the area north of Plymouth.

More frequently seen are managed woodlands, some sadly neglected. In many broadleaved woods the oak and ash are mixed with sweet chestnut, beech, sycamore, rowan, alder, hawthorn and blackthorn, elder, holly and hazel. You will also see blocks of softwoods - the technical description of timber which comes from evergreen trees, not necessarily a true reflection of its hardness. Yew, for instance, is a hard wood, though it comes from an evergreen tree and is therefore described as a softwood. (Elder is a soft wood, but technically because it comes from a deciduous tree, is a hardwood.) Most frequently found in churchyards, some yew trees are very ancient, and it is not unknown for them to be a thousand years old. It is salutary to reflect that the tree you stand beside could have been alive when Elizabeth I was Queen, might have been planted when the building of the church was started, or possibly was already growing when the Domesday Book was compiled by the conquering Norman Barons. There are several magnificent yews of varying age in the grounds of Dartington Hall, near Totnes, solitary and grouped.

It is because on the whole we absorb the pattern of forest growth as random around the source of seeds, that we find the ranks of single species planting so alien when we are faced with it in blocks of managed woodland. There are fashions in this, as in other things, and you will notice that some woods have dark stands of evergreens in geometrically precise formation, which rather than bringing rhythm by their uniformity, shriek against the harmony of natural regeneration with its mixed textures, colours and sizes. Both have a place, and it is important that we learn from each. Now that an increasing number of community woodlands are being established, by planting, donation or purchase, we shall have the opportunity to explore and enjoy different kinds of woodland and to understand why each looks as it does.

Rural South Hams.

Interest is growing in the management of woodland for sustainability. Perhaps the oldest technique of this sort is coppicing, and several neglected hazel coppices in the area are being regenerated. Coppicing secures a constant renewal of new growth which the tree is stimulated into providing by being cut back when harvesting wood of the size needed for hurdles, gates, furniture, and all the many uses of hazel. The South Hams Environment Trust, the District Council Environment Service, the Devon Wildlife Trust and the Woodland Trust - now a national organisation, but started locally - are all involved in this work, as is the International Tree Foundation, perhaps better known by its former, more romantic though less politically correct title, 'Men of the Trees'. It is not possible to travel the South Hams without at some time using the deep set lanes, their banks topped by hedges in the combination which is so characteristic of the region. In the Spring and Summer, the steep banks are vivid with a succession of wildflowers, primroses, celandine and violet, followed by bluebells, campion, dandelions, buttercups, Queen Anne's lace, meadowsweet, goosegrass and a host of others, on through the Autumn. The policy for managing the roadside verges now allows them to seed before cutting, and on wide corners you will notice a swathe of grass cut for road safety purposes, while the rest grows on to maturity. This is speedily restoring the richness to our wildflower population and provides food for insects such as butterflies and moths, both as caterpillars and mature insects, and bees and birds. It also creates more of the wildlife corridors on which a healthy local flora and fauna depend.

The verges change colour as the year moves on, from the bright yellow of Spring, through the blues, pinks and whites of Summer, until the dandelions and the brown seed heads are left to contrast with the red or purple berries of woody and deadly nightshade, and the creaming froth of wild clematis, 'old man's beard', winding its way along, over and down, everything.

Some of the best sources of wildflowers in variety are churchyards. The villages of the South Hams have ancient Parish Churches, many of them built between the thirteenth and fifteenth centuries. The churchyards have not been subjected to the use of pesticides, weedkillers and fertilisers, and so they are refuges for the birds, insects and small mammals which rely on many species which have been lost elsewhere. Churchyard management schemes which cut the grass only at carefully selected times and leave some parts undisturbed altogether are not a sign of neglect or disrespect to those buried there, but a symbol of hope for the future as we try to regenerate some of the former richness which those earlier generations took for granted.

Please remember that wildflowers should not be picked. Many are protected by law, but all wild growing things should gain their strongest protection from our own desire to preserve them.

The deep South Hams enjoy a climate which ensures flowers grow here long after they have faded in the less favoured parts. The climate is largely a product of the warm sea current, the Gulf Stream, which surrounds the area and seems to keep the clouds at bay so that there are more sunshine hours here, as well as higher temperatures. Foreign visitors such as oranges and eucalyptuses grow near Salcombe, where frost is almost unheard of.

The climate and underlaying rocks together produce the soil of an area, and it is evident that the land here is rich growing country. The large native breeds of cattle, the South Devons and Red Ruby originated here, and the splendid local livestock can be admired at the many agricultural shows which vividly reflect local life and interests, around the area throughout the Summer, following the splendours of the Devon County Show in May.

The dairy industry supports the new growth in local cheesemaking and ice cream manufacture as well as the clotted cream for which Devon is famous. Corn is grown, and the green of the pastures is chequered with golden fields of wheat and barley in Summer. Very occasionally you may see among the fields of large round bales, a field with stooks of corn looking like a film set, or a farm in a time warp. Devon cottages are often thatched with 'combed wheat reed', which is not a reed at all, but thatching straw. This has to be grown without the aid of artifical fertilisers, which make the straw too soft so that it does not last on the roof, and it cannot be cut by a combine-harvester, but needs an old fashioned cutter. To keep the length of straw and the single direction of lay, it is still bound in stooks, so that the thatchers can use it easily.

The skills of thatching are thriving once again, which is good news for the owners of those calendar-picture cottages which are so characteristic of the South West, and this area in particular. Thatch is light, an excellent insulator both for sound and heat and, unlike the alternatives, clay or plastic tiles or slates, is a renewable resource.

Look for the repaired roof ridges and patches to the corners exposed to the prevailing wind and weather, and the ornaments to the roof ridge - sometimes birds such as pheasants, sometimes stylized shapes - which are the individual thatcher's signature to his work. It is hard to remember that not so long ago, thatch was the cheap and easy roofing material, the skill available to all farm workers, used to roof the lowliest of sheds and to protect every haystack from the weather.

Thatch is usually, but not inevitably, teamed up with cob, the mud mix building material which gives that delightful rounded look to the oldest cottages, houses and farm buildings. Cob is strong and durable; many of the buildings we admire today originated in Tudor times and have withstood over four hundred years of weather and living. It is made from puddled mud mixed with organic material such as straw. Often an old farmyard will show the depression at one end, sometimes still used as the duckpond, sometimes paved over, which is where the cob for the farmbuildings was made.

The cob was laid on top of a stone plinth which keeps the water from the base of it, and had a generous overhang at the eaves (easy if it was thatched) so that the mud was kept dry. The outside walls are weatherproofed by render, often with local clays to give a white, pink or deep cream finish. So long as cob walls have dry feet and a good bonnet, as the saying goes, they are good for a hundred years. Keep an eye open for the occasional farmyard wall built of cob, with a tiled (and very rarely, thatched) top, an unusual but by no means entirely unfamiliar sight.

The other common roofing materials are clay tiles, usually red, and slate. Slate was a local product, so some slate roofs are very old in the South Hams, whereas in other areas they had to wait until the railways allowed Welsh slate to be brought in. You may notice older houses where the roof was once thatched, where the gables stand proud of the present roof line, because the slates are so much thinner than the deep thatch cover they replaced.

In the Dartmoor villages you will notice more stone building. The granite was plentiful, though hard to work. Particularly attractive is the combination of darkly sparkling granite and rounded golden thatch which can be seen in some areas. The straighter lines of the walls give away the stone under the colourwash, more suited to this wetter, harsher climate.

Many of the villages and towns of the South Hams have very old origins. There are Bronze Age settlements and Iron Age hill forts in the District. The Romans were not much in evidence in this remote area; place names are largely Saxon, and many churches bear the record of foundation at the time of the Saxon Invasion. The towns and villages share the concern to preserve their special character. Dartmouth, Kingsbridge, Modbury, South Brent, are busy and attractive centres for their localities, with fascinating histories, all well worth wandering round at leisure.

The ecosystem of village life is every bit as delicate and capable of being unbalanced as any other. A petrol station attached to a new supermarket might eventually lead to the closure of several local garages, causing the loss of the mechanic who repairs machinery of all kinds. The free bus from the superstore attracts the former customers of the village shop. The post office closes because the government encourages people to take their benefits through bank accounts. The farm shop closes because of milk regulations, and a thousand and one other regulations, and the families move away, so the school closes, and the pub gets into difficulties, and gradually you will find holiday homes called 'The Old School House' or 'The Old Post Office', or 'The Old Red Lion', and 'The Old Vicarage' making up a carefully tended but dead group of attractive buildings. They are as much a 'village'as a body on a life-support system is a person. The pattern is repeated all over the country. Until we recognise that regenerating rural areas with people who live there permanently should be the major priority of our economic, social and environmental policies, we shall see continuing decay eating away at what was not so long ago the source of the nation's wealth. The result will be a countryside which is no more than a sanitised rural theme park, to be experienced, looked at, photographed, and shut up until next summer. Happily, in the South Hams this is beginning to be reversed.

A visit to the museum in the smaller towns will provide an interesting insight into how the landscape of the town and surrounding country came to look as they do today. The environment is after all, a collective word expressing the totality of the land, sea, water, air and buildings which surround us.

In the South Hams, the landscape has largely been shaped by agriculture, principally stock farming. The underlying rocks are some of the oldest on Earth. The Devonian Period in geological terms takes its name from the county, where these rock types were first studied. Containing some of the earliest fossils of land-based vertebrates, they were laid down about 400 million years ago, when South America, Africa and India were still all one great land mass.

The oldest rocks in Devon, the Lower Devonian deposits, lie exposed between Bolt Tail and Start Point, horn blende and mica schists. In bands running West to East across the rest of the district, more Lower Devonian deposits in the form of sandstones and slates are found, followed by Middle Devonian slates ('middle' as in a sandwich filling - laid on top of the lower layer of rock). Perhaps the quickest way to observe the changing rock type is to notice what the village church is built of.

The northern area of South Hams, on Dartmoor, has granite outcrops, the decayed granite forming the china clay which is extracted in the area around

Cornwood and Shaugh Prior. A startling 'lunar' landscape results, similar to the area around Newton Abbot, or St. Austell in Cornwall. A valuable resource, it is exported all over the world. The area is well worth a visit to see the effect of human activity on the landscape, and to enjoy the stunning panorama out over Plymouth Sound. Many interesting varieties of bird which are not found in the lowland areas can be seen here, dependent on the heath and scrub which provide a contrast in habitat, equally as important as the softer landscape to the South.

There are many lime kilns still in evidence in the South Hams, though it has little local limestone. Neighbouring Torbay and Plymouth have considerable areas. There is evidence of the volcanic activity which was once a major factor in the shaping of the South West. Although not in the South Hams, North Brentor is worth noting. St. Michael's Church is perched on a curious cone-shaped hill, reminiscent of the Tor at Glastonbury, which is also crowned by a St. Michael's Church. Both are volcanic plugs, reminders of the exciting forces which once worked on the rocks of these parts.

The economic activity of human beings has shaped the landscape since nature did its major work. Mineral extraction such as the clay mining and quarrying have been important for a very long time. Quarries of stone and slate can be seen throughout the district, some small, for local building, some much larger. Most are no longer used. This creates an environmental problem in that stone detailing on new buildings, repairs to old ones, or garden work, cannot easily be carried out in local, appropriate stone. So often, good intentions evidenced by using stone for a wall or extension or a new property, are marred by the use of 'foreign' stone which defeats the purpose. Instead of the property seeming to share a link with other properties in the area, it looks out of place. Often this is not the fault of the owner, who simply cannot buy appropriate stone, and did not realise that the next village produces a wildly different variety in colour and texture. Our town planners and architects should stipulate with precision what must be used, or accept that it is no longer available, and reject the stone in favour of a rendered finish which would in fact blend in better.

The good news environmentally is that following the closure of quarries, their steep, difficult of access walls provide undisturbed habitat for many wild species and the bottom will often furnish a wetland area, desperately needed in these days of farmers draining their land and increasing areas being placed under roads and buildings. More pools, bogs and soggy areas would be the best news for wildlife in most areas.

The South Hams is an area of varied and valuable environmental importance. This ranges from the efforts to keep villages as living communities, to the protection of areas where such endangered species as the cirl bunting live. The south of the district has a large proportion of the native population of this small brown bird. There are populations of plants, even worms, which are of major significance, and they are found in small woods, the beds of the estuaries, corners of fields, and often look quite unremarkable. Much work is being done to study this precious resource, and to find out precisely what treasures the region holds. It is then necessary to conserve and protect what we find.

The maxim 'Think globally, act locally' applies here, as everywhere. You will find that in the South Hams a lot of effort has produced a network of recycling facilities which is remarkable for such a scattered population and small authority. Everthing from ozone threatening CFCs out of scrap refrigerators, through used engine oil, to aluminium drinks cans and glass of every kind, can be dealt with at a relatively local centre. If you are visiting, please use the bottle banks and can banks; you are in a area which recycles more glass per head of population than anywhere else. Please help us to keep our reputation. Those of use who live, play or work anywhere on this extraordinary planet need to be aware of the need to conserve its precious resources. We who are privilged to enjoy the South Hams must bear our responsibility not only for ourselves, but on behalf of all those children not yet born, who, but for a decision of ours about what to do, or not to do, what to buy or not to buy, may never enjoy the wonder of a badger lumbering across the road, a frog startling them beside a damp path, or a red deer lifting its magnificent head to taste the wind.

For the long legs of the heron, the sunshine of the cowslip, the silken carpet of a dewy September morning woven by new spiders; the grisled glory of an old oak; the athletic silver of a leaping salmon; the furry coat of trailing lichen, the sinister gleam of fungi, all these wonders are part of what we can enjoy if we are aware. Listen - to ravens, larks and blackbirds; to bees and foxes. Smell meadowsweet and stinkhorn. Look at everything closely, from a dandelion head to the sweep of a cliff and the curve of the river.

Enjoy them, and determine to do whatever you can to keep them. Take only photographs, leave only footprints. Think of the consequences of what you do. Then the extraordinarily rich environment of the South Hams will continue to be here to enjoy, not only for ourselves in the future, but for other generations, the rest of whose world we cannot begin to imagine.

Royal Seven Stars Hotel

TOTNES. SOUTH DEVON. Tel: (01803) 862125 / 863241

It is fitting that Totnes, one of England's most ancient boroughs, should have a hotel with the character and atmosphere of the famed Royal Seven Stars. Built in 1660, during the restoration of the monarchy, it has been a part of the history of Totnes throughout the centuries. The hotel has eighteen bedrooms, most of which are en suite, and equipped with colour televisions, direct-dial phones, beverage tray and central heating. The Royal Seven Stars has a fine reputation for food, and has facilities for weddings, parties, receptions, dinner-dances, conferences and meetings of all descriptions. There are special banquetting menus, and special weekend breaks throughout the year, and the hotel offers live entertainment from time to time. Ken Stone, the General Manager has run the hotel since 1963 and has maintained standards of excellence which are rarely equalled. Private parking for 20 cars. Mastercard and Visa accepted. Dogs permitted. An ideal situation for exploring Dartmoor and the South Hams.

Riverford
FARM SHOP
RIVERFORD. STAVERTON. TOTNES.
Telephone: (01803) 762523

The Watson family has farmed the 500 acre Riverford Farm for over forty years, ten of which have been spent working to bring back the taste and quality of traditional country foods. Organically reared meat, home cured bacon, organic vegetables and fruit - here is excellence indeed. Pies and pates, port-cured ham, poultry and game ... and sausages which are ... well you will just have to try them! Wine and cider too. If you want produce that tastes as it used to this is the place to find it.

MEMBER OF THE
SOUTH HAMS FOOD &
DRINK ASSOCIATION

PENNYWELL

FARM & WILDLIFE CENTRE

BUCKFASTLEIGH.   Telephone: (01364) 642023

If you have a family to entertain - whatever their ages - I can think of no finer place to spend the best part of a day than this superb working farm, which has been specifically designed with children in mind. To see and do everything can take nearly six hours; there are ponies to ride, goats to milk, baby lambs to feed, donkeys to groom, nature trails to walk, pigs to scratch (yes - really) and a host of other distractions to keep the entire family entertained, amused and reminding what life is all about. The views from Pennywell are spectacular and the air is like wine, but the real sight to see is the face of a child who is meeting a 'Bambi' for the first time! There is an owl and falconry centre - a 'hands-on' experience where you can be shown how to fly a barn owl or buzzard. I doubt there is a more rewarding experience than to visit Pennywell. The staff are friendly and helpful - they are trained to use their skills to help the children know and understand animals, yet at the same time there is nothing in any way patronising about the way in which this 'education' is imparted. Love of the creatures - both animal and human must be the secret. The new Dartmoor Farmhouse Kitchen provides everything from snacks to full meals, such as steak and kidney pie, and cousin Jeremy's cakes and scones are a knockout!

Facilities for parties and functions are available, by arrangement with owners Chris and Nicky Murray. Shop, picnic area, lecture rooms .... Pennywell has it all. Most highly recommended. Triple award winner; as seen on BBC TV. Woody's Award of Excellence.

QUALITY PRODUCE
SOUTH HAMS

MEMBER OF THE
SOUTH HAMS FOOD &
DRINK ASSOCIATION

The Old Church House Inn

TORBRYAN. IPPLEPEN. S. DEVON. Telephone: (01803) 812372

This ancient graded inn goes back to Saxon times, but most of the inn dates from the 14th Century. An inn for all seasons, it has ten lovely en suite bedrooms, and has earned four crowns and commendation from the English Tourist Board. Log fires in woodburners, lanterns and beams and stonework create an intimate timeless atmosphere of romance and history. Henry VIII stayed here, and Cromwell used this building as his headquarters! The food is first class - they can seat over 100 guests, ideal for weddings, parties and all functions. Featured in numerous films - there is even a replica in Los Angeles! Mastercard/Visa welcome - as are children. Featured in all worthwhile guides. Superb a la carte menu and daily specials. Real Ales. A cracker!

The Tally-Ho!

LITTLEHEMPSTON. NR. TOTNES. DEVON.   Telephone: (01803) 862316

This lovely 14th Century Inn is one of Devon's 'gems' and has received many accolades for its superb food and atmosphere. Featured in the good beer guide, and recommended by C.A.M.R.A., the inn has three Real Ales, a fine wine list and the selection of food ranges from bar snacks, sandwiches, basket meals and daily specials right through to a full a la carte menu featuring fresh fish from Brixham, poultry, game and meat all prepared with flair by chef Steve Germon. A lovely garden, featuring a flower-filled patio and lawn with ornamental borders, and tables and chairs enabling you to enjoy eating outdoors. Highly recommended. No credit cards; large car park.

The Monk's Retreat

THE SQUARE. BROADHEMPSTON. NR. TOTNES.
Telephone: (01803) 812203

This lovely inn is a true Devon hostelry which dates back to the 15th century. Apart from Mondays, when it is closed all day, the inn is open every day of the week, and offers some of the best home-cooking to be found anywhere. Known as the 'Small Pub with the Large Menu', the Monk's Retreat has something for everyone. Steak on a Stone is a house speciality. You cook it yourself on a hot stone at the table - complete with dips. Potatoes and accompanying dishes for the steaks arrive pre-cooked and ready to eat. This is a fun way to eat especially in a large jovial party.

The extensive - but NOT expensive menu includes super home-made soups, fresh fish, pies, casseroles + Sunday roasts. Daily specials are displayed on various blackboards and include local, British, Foreign + Vegetarian Foods. Many home-made desserts and local ice creams are also available, all topped with delicious Devonshire Clotted Cream. Your hosts are Alan and Theresa Lidstone, and it is their choice of Real Ales, guest beers, good wines + planning that has created the warm atmosphere and hospitality of a true Devon Country Inn.

Complete with its large log fires it has a resident Ghost! Reported to be that of a Monk, incense can be detected in the air when he is around. This is particularly noticeable on Christmas Eve - so if it affects the smell of the delicious Roast turkey - then YOU have ever right to be incensed.

BUCKFAST ABBEY

he monks of Buckfast welcome visitors to their famous Abbey, set in the wooded valley of the River Dart, within the Dartmoor National Park. Founded in 1018, closed at the Reformation, the Abbey lay in ruins until monks returned in 1882. The present Abbey Church took just four of the monks thirty-two years to rebuild, and contains many art treasures, including magnificent stained glass windows made in the Abbey workshops. Recently, restoration work has continued on the many fine medieval buildings in the precinct. Today's community is engaged in farming, beekeeping, winemaking and craftwork but above all, the Abbey remains a spiritual centre and retains an extraordinary tranquillity: few visitors leave untouched by the peace and serenity of Buckfast.

The monks sell their own tonic wine, honey and pottery in the Abbey Shop, and there is also an exhibition, video, restaurant and bookshop.

The Abbey is half a mile from the A38 at Buckfastleigh.

Buckfast Abbey, Buckfastleigh,
Devon TQ11 0EE ☎ 01364 642519
Buckfast Abbey is a registered charity.

Holne Chase Hotel and Restaurant

Nr. ASHBURTON · DEVON · TQ13 7NS   **Telephone: (01364) 631471**

Back in 1849 White's Directory of Devon described Holne Chase House as being in 'A Singularly Secluded and Romantic Situation". There is no reason to change this description in 1995. Mary and Kenneth Bromage have run Holne Chase since 1972. The award winning Restaurant, with an extensive but sensibly priced wine list, is open daily for Lunch and Dinner. Please telephone to ensure availability, particularly at weekends. Many regulars come for Morning Coffee or a Light Lunch off the interesting "Snack" menu or for the Traditional Devon Cream Tea for which the Hotel is renowned.

Holne Chase is a popular venue for weddings so the "House Full" sign may be found from time to time. A telephone call is always worth while.

Morning Coffee from 10.00 am, Bar Snacks from noon to 2.00 pm, Restaurant Lunch 12.30 pm to 1.45 pm - £14.50 inc. VAT. Afternoon Tea 3.00 pm to 5.00 pm (Devon Cream Tea £3.50). Dinner 7.15pm to 9.00pm - £21.00 and A La Carte. Terrace Service April to October subject to climatic conditions (not dinner). Open fires in Public Rooms when seasonal. Prices correct at time of going to press.

TOTNES

Totnes is an extraordinary town and no one will argue that it is as good a place as any to start the exploration of this enchanting area. It is the second oldest borough in England, next only to Chester. Its streets and buildings, the riverside development, and its castle set out the history of urban living over a thousand years. The Totnes and District Society work to spread knowledge of the town, and useful leaflets are available from their office in the High Street, or the Tourist Information Office in the Plains. Much excellent work has been carried out by the Totnes & District Preservation Society, which continues to acquire important buildings suffering from neglect and conserve them, restoring them to active use. A recent acquisition is the Town Mill, near Safeway Supermarket, which seems to have been unique, being driven by two water wheels, one powered by the leat which served several mills along this stretch, the other wheel being tidally driven. Several organisations are working together to secure the future of this historic building.

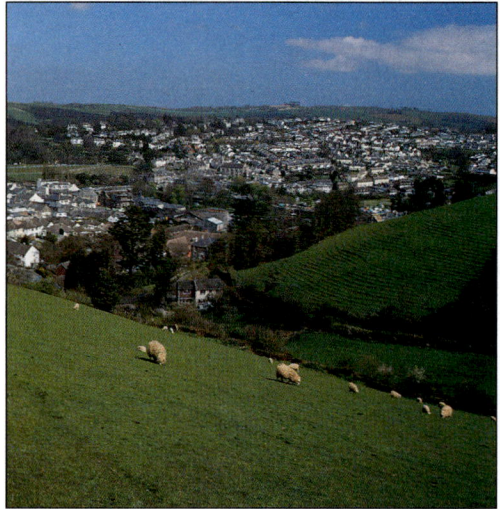

When so many towns are indistinguisable from one another because of modern building styles and materials, and the march of the national chains of shops which insist on having the same shop front and agressively individual modern signwriting on their establishments however inappropriate in scale, colour or style they may be to their surroundings, it is refreshing to visit a town like Totnes (and there are very few) where the modern world is kept in place behind the charming street frontages. The town is built on a hill rising from the banks of the River Dart, extending to the suburb of Bridgetown. The first mention of it is made during the reign of Edgar in AD 959 when coins were minted here, but its unique magic is distilled from its age and beauty with the fascinating little lanes leading from its one main street, a hotch potch of building periods, much like the ups and downs of its fortunes.

Apart from the busiest periods at the height of the holiday season Totnes offers the visitor ample car parking, and as it is a town best explored on foot we recommend using a car park and let the car stay put. Probably as good a one to choose as any is the Steamer Quay, found on the opposite side of the river Dart to that of the town itself. From here boat trips to Dartmouth, taking in the pleasures of the Dart on the way, of which greater mention will be given later, begin their journey. Alongside Steamer Quay stands the Totnes Motor Museum, run by Richard and Trisha Pilkington, the latter well known for her days as a Grand Prix driver. Here you can see everything from an Austin 7 to an Aston Martin. The boat trips and motor museum are only open and operating during the holiday season, and toilet/refreshment facilities are available.

Leaving Steamer Quay and walking back over the old road bridge to Totnes, which incidentally is the lowest crossing point on the river Dart, Vire Island lies to the left. It is a small landscaped island offering seating and picnic areas, and is named after the town of that name in Normandy, with which Totnes was twinned in 1973. The South Hams has a long standing relationship with this part of France, for it was from around here that such a vast number of the allied D.Day invasion force departed.

The statue standing in the middle of the road in the Plains area is of William John Wills, erected in 1864 by public subscription. With a man named Burke he was the first to cross the Australian continent. Born in 1834 he went to work in Australia and eventually got a job in an observatory in Melbourne. Through this he became engaged in 1860 as a surveyor with an exhibition crossing the then unexplored interior of Australia. Burke was the leader, a man not blessed with the best of luck, and one prone to making vital mistakes. True to form Burke's party ran out of water on the return journey and all but one, including Wills, perished.

The Plains have seen more change than any other part of Totnes. Once an area where many ships carrying timber and other goods docked, with warehouses and yards lining the bank of the river, it now proudly boasts new houses, shops and businesses, many converted from the old warehouses. The National Trust shop occupies the ground floor of a former Merchant's house. On the other side of the Plains stands the little Dartmouth Inn Square with a refurbished pub and flats. A fountain at the head of the Square was erected here in May 1988 having previously stood in Station Road since 1904 to commemorate Queen Victoria's Diamond Jubilee.

Alongside is Ticklemore Street with a variety of shops including a superb fishmongers. Nearby is the Tourist Information Centre where further detailed reference of Totnes and its attractions can be obtained.

Fore Street and then High Street run up and through the centre of Totnes. At the bottom of Fore Street stands the Royal Seven Stars Hotel, the history of which would make a book in itself. It dates back to the mid 17th century - the days of coach and horses. The hotel once had a courtyard through which the horses passed to the stables at the rear. This is now covered in and part of the hall and reception area. Daniel Defoe, author of 'Robinson Crusoe and Moll Flanders' stayed here whilst researching his book 'A Tour of England and Wales' published during 1724. The Totnes town trail starts from this point.

Just up the hill from here is the old post office, built in 1928 with a roof and face hung with slates, as are so many of the houses in this town. The post office is now sited in Forbuoys Newsagents, just a few yards further on. Four doors up from Station Road is found the Brutus Stone, look carefully, for it is easily missed. It is said that Brutus, the Trojan coloniser of Britain, set foot on this stone when he first came ashore at Totnes.

A little further up on the opposite side is the Elizabethan House Town Museum, built around 1575 for Walter Kelland a local merchant. There is a cobbled courtyard, the rooms are high and airy, featuring displays of childrens' games and clothes, dolls' houses, and furniture, alongside Victorian Valentines, bygones from the Great Western Railway, an old time grocer's shop, the story of W.J. Wills, mentioned earlier, and that of Charles Babbage who invented the Babbage Analytical Engine, an early 19th century forerunner of the computer. He also invented the 'Cow Catcher', first fitted to the front of steam engines in the days of the Wild West to keep the line clear. This is still used in many parts of the world. The spiral staircase in the building is well worn by generations of feet of Totnes residents, it encircles a huge pole said to be the mast from an Elizabeth ship.

The most noticeable feature of Totnes is the Eastgate Arch which spans the

main street. It was recently destroyed by fire, which resulted in this end of the road being closed to traffic whilst it was perfectly and lovingly restored. Eastgate is owned by the Duke of Somerset, who also owns Berry Pomeroy and Bridgetown. From beneath the arch a flight of steps and a path sign-posted Ramparts Walk, leads to the 16th century Guildhall Yard. The Guildhall was built in 1553 and is open weekdays between Easter and October. On display inside are the Mayor's parlour, the town's jail cells and its constitutional history. Opposite is the lovely old church of St. Marys with its 120 foot red sandstone tower. The organ is part of the one built for the Great Exhibition of 1851, and the rood screen is formed of Beer stone from east Devon.

Returning to the main street the visitor soon comes to the Butterwalk, the name derived from the fact that butter and cheeses had to be kept in the cool shade during the summer months when these were sold in the open market. Most of the buildings around here are again slate hung, built in the 16th and 17th centuries. Among them is Bogan House, no. 43 High Street, one of the most interesting and historical houses in Totnes, and the home of beautiful displays of costumes and accessories. Opposite the Butterwalk is the Civic Hall fronted by a market square, which every Tuesday during the summer months boasts a re-creation of days past.

During the reign of Henry VIII the town was second only in importance and wealth to Exeter and this lasted through the Elizabethan Age. Traders and townsfolk dress in Elizabethan costume, creating a lively and colourful spectacle. On these Elizabethan Tuesdays the Town's stocks are on display in the market square and are a must for the visitor's photo albums, especially as they can be 'tried out for size'.

The High Street carries on around a corner but a lane off to the right leads to the remains of the Norman castle on a mound rising to 50 feet, and crowned with a small stone keep. The Castle is open all year round and is maintained by English Heritage. Around the corner of the High Street sign-posts direct visitors to the Leechwells. Three stone troughs are fed by jets of water coming from holes in the wall. These have flowed for generations and are said to cure many ills, the name probably arising from the description of a doctor in olden times as a Leech. The three troughs are known as snake, toad and long cripple (grass snake). The Leechwells are found a hundred yards or so down a narrow lane leading off to the left of the Kingsbridge Inn, which is reckoned to be the oldest inn in Totnes.

Having explored Totnes on foot the visitor may now like to take in some of the pleasures of the river Dart. The river is navigable to Totnes with a weir two miles up stream, the limit of the tidal water, above which is only fresh water from the moor. A favourite trip is to sail down the Dart from the Totnes Steamer Quay in one of the many pleasure boats which go to Dartmouth, passing some wonderful scenery. It has been compared with the Rhine in Germany. During the voyage you pass such places of interest as Agatha Christie's house and Bow Creek, near which a famous television chef runs a pub - Floyd's Inn (Sometimes). From this quay at the time of the Armada the Crescent and Hart

joined the fleet in Plymouth, and Totnes contributed to their outfit. The town also co-operated in the Second World War when a number of minesweepers were built of wood here to safeguard them from magnetic mines. Amphibious landing craft were provided for the invasion of Normandy, and corvettes floated down river to have their engines fitted at Dartmouth before being hidden away in the estuary creek until they were needed.

The railway came to Totnes in 1847 and in 1872 a branch line through the Dart Valley to Buckfastleigh was opened. However, along with many others at the time this line was closed during 1958, but thanks to local railway enthusiasts, visitors and locals alike can now once again ride on the steam journey along the seven miles of track beside the beautiful river Dart. At the Buckfastleigh end of the line is situated the South Devon Railway's main base, where a large collection of locomotives and carriages is housed. Mention must also be made of the Butterfly Farm and Otter Sanctuary, situated alongside the Buckfastleigh railway station.

Inevitably Totnes is linked with Dartington, and although it is not possible to walk the whole of the way from Totnes along the river bank, you can pick up the path the other side of the railway station by walking across the school

playing fields where the leat runs under the oak trees and past vegetable gardens in neat rows. Seagulls dive and scream over the weir and in the tranquil water above you may see a skiff being rowed by young men who could be on the Cambridge Backs, except the willows are missing. The water is completely placid between meadows dotted with ancient oaks where cattle graze. Now and then the surface is broken by a leaping fish or a pair of stately swans. Above here, at the end of a drive, stands Dartington Hall, its history going back into the mists of time, the first recorded Saxon settlement west of Exeter. This history is a combination of money, inheritance, but above all, idealism, the dream of Leonard Elmhirst and his American wife, Dorothy Witney Straight, who bought the estate in 1925 with the vision of a self-financing rural community and established a Trust in 1931. Leonard had met Tagore, Indian poet, novelist and essayist, and gone to Bengal to set up an Institute of Rural Reconstruction, hence Dartington. The idealism of the Elmhirsts could be said to be the blueprint for the welfare state for many of the men and women who laid the foundations of post war Britain came first to Dartington to observe, and went away with a vision of a better world. However for many years the whole project and the people involved were looked upon with great suspicion by the Devonians with all the talk of communism and free love. The Trust first of all founded a co-educational school and went on to encompass many activities from farm and dairy, textiles, shops and forestry, a College of Arts offering full time courses in music and drama, and residential courses in various subjects.

The Amadeus String Quartet was formed here, and the potter Bernard Leach taught at the Arts Centre as did Henry Moore. The Elmhirsts funded a then unknown playwright R. C. Sherrif and his play 'Journey's End' which became a sell out in the West End. In 1944 they opened a Cattle Breeding Centre making artificial insemination available to hundreds of farmers who didn't want to keep their own bulls.

Here now a prestigious literary seminar is held annually, 'Way with Words' with such speakers as Ruth Rendell, Mary Wesley etc. The gardens are free and open to all. The Hall was built in 1388 by John Holland, half brother to King Richard II, and is said to be the most spectacular mediaeval mansion in Devon with a quadrangle that has hardly changed over the centuries, and a great central hall with a hammer beam roof. The Champernowne family lived here from 1559 until the present century, but owing to financial ruin brought about by the agricultural recession the estate had to be broken up and sold when the Elmhirsts bought it.

For 600 years or more the house was occupied keeping an air of continuity and tranquillity, a distillation of the magic of Devon. In the garden the trees, contours, lawns and flowering shrubs create shadows and shapes which bring endless delight and in the centre is the tilting yard, its terraces crowned with

Spanish chestnut trees at least 400 years old. At the bottom of the glade is Henry Moore's figure of a reclining woman which he put there in 1947. He wrote that he wanted the figure to have … "The quiet stillness, and sense of permanence as though it would stay there forever - as though it had come to terms with the world and could get over the largest care and losses." Do not miss the enchanting donkey in bronze by Willi Soukop, or the 12 tall yew trees representing Apostles round the tiltyard. At Shinners Bridge is the Dartington Cider Press Centre, a complex of shops and restaurants, famous for exhibitions by some of the finest British craftsmen - unusual toys, Dartington Crystal, herbs and spices, farm food, a kitchen shop, street theatre, music, dancing clowns and demonstrations all set in beautiful surroundings.

A short drive from Totnes off the Kingsbridge road is Bowden House, which like most Manor houses has a somewhat chequered career. It dates back to the 9th century and at one time was the residence of the De Broase family, builders of the 13th century Totnes Castle mentioned earlier. It also boasts a ghost or two and 'ghost tours' are conducted. In the adjoining complex are a photographic museum with more than 1,000 old cameras and an enormous collection of photographs, and a cafe. Bowden House and its attractions are open from early to late season on Mondays, Tuesdays, Wednesdays, Thursdays and Bank Holiday Sundays.

Dartbridge Inn

TOTNES ROAD. BUCKFASTLEIGH. Tel: (01364) 642214

One of the most popular - and most photographed Inns in the West Country, the Dartbridge Inn is famous for its magnificent floral displays. Situated on the banks of the river Dart, the inn is renowned for good food, with an extensive a la carte menu, and daily blackboard 'specials' offering pheasant, veal, guinea fowl and many other delicacies. A typical table d'hote menu gives you a choice of five starters (home-made soup, deep fried camembert, avocado vinaigrette, cornets of hams and asparagus or chilled fruit juice.) Main courses include fricassee of veal, lamb casserole with rosemary, poached cod in mushroom cream and white wine sauce. Functions room for up to 100 and superb facilities for weddings, private parties etc.

The Sea Trout Inn

STAVERTON. TOTNES. DEVON.   Telephone: (01803) 762274

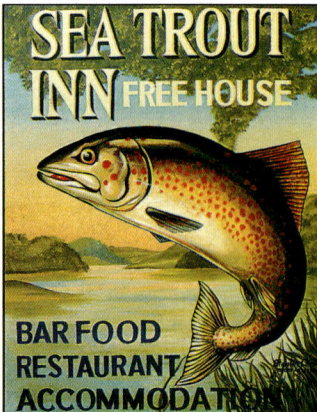

Dating from the 15th century this superb inn is a free house, owned and run by Pym and Andrew Mogford. There are ten fine bedrooms, all en suite, with colour TV, direct dial telephone, central heating and tea/coffee facilities. Exceptional menus with wide choice of fare, all home-cooked, and daily blackboard specials. Examples: Breast of chicken filled with stilton and celery with port wine and mushroom sauce. Real Ales and a good choice of wines, and all at reasonable prices. A true Devon Inn - and one of Woody's top selections!

MEMBER OF THE
SOUTH HAMS FOOD &
DRINK ASSOCIATION

FINGALS

OLD COOMBE MANOR FARM
DITTISHAM
DARTMOUTH
TQ6 0JA

Telephone: 01803 722398

Fingals is different! It is a hotel …… but let me quote from the owner's comments in the hotel brochure. "Fingals is not a straightforward hotel. It is a special place with an atmosphere and personality of its own. The style is informal and easy going. Nobody will be upset if you sleep in and want breakfast at ten o'clock. There is no need to dress for dinner, and surnames are dispensed with". These comments only tell half the story. Fingals is a delight. Idyllic setting in a valley just a mile from the picturesque village of Dittisham, amidst landscaped gardens and vine-draped verandahs, here you can enjoy country pursuits such as trout fishing …… and return to a swim in the heated pool, or have a sauna and jacuzzi! Fine food, tennis, croquet. This is quality.

QUALITY PRODUCE · SOUTH HAMS

MEMBER OF THE
SOUTH HAMS FOOD &
DRINK ASSOCIATION

Crowdy Mill

BOW ROAD. HARBERTONFORD.
TOTNES. DEVON. TQ9 7HU

Tel: (01803) 732340

This fine example of a 17th century working watermill stands on the banks of the river Harbourne, and produces two tonnes of organic wheat flour every week, supplying restaurants and health food shops throughout the westcountry. The cafe is open from April to November, serving the best Devon Cream Teas you are ever likely to find. Bed and breakfast in the Mill cottage (with en suite bathrooms) or self catering in converted barns. Lovely countryside to explore, and excellent home-cooked food at the Mill. Much sought after. Take a look at the comments in the visitors book!

MEMBER OF THE
SOUTH HAMS FOOD &
DRINK ASSOCIATION

THE DARTMOUTH INN

WARLAND · TOTNES · **Telephone: (01803) 863252**

This handsome inn is one of three which are owned and run by Andrew Milton. Outside tables under broad-leaved trees in this quiet square are part of the charm of the Dartmouth Inn, and the interior is equally delightful. Open from 11.00 a.m. to 11.00 p.m., the inn serves food from 12.00 - 2.30 p.m. and, during the summer, from 6.00 p.m. to 9.30 p.m. (Winter, Friday and Saturday only). Basket meals, filled jacket potatoes and steak & kidney pie are some of the dishes available. The Watermans is Andrew's other Totnes pub, and in Kingsbridge it is The Quay. No credit cards

33

The Kingsbridge Inn

9 Leechwell Street. Totnes. Devon. TQ9 5SY
Telephone (01803) 863324
Licensees Rosemary Triggs. Martyn and Jane Canevali.

FREE HOUSE
* EGON RONAY GOOD PUB GUIDE RECOMMENDED
* PUBLICAN MAGAZINE PUB RED WINE OF THE YEAR 1993-1994
* SOUTH DEVON CAMRA PUB OF THE YEAR 1993

Mentioned in the Domesday Book (1086). This fine inn has a 17th century ghost! She can only be seen, it appears, by females. However really excellent food can be enjoyed by both sexes, so let's concentrate on the substance not the shadow. Kingsbridge Inn gained Woody's Award of Excellence for the selection, preparation and presentation of food and wine, as well as other accolades. Real Ales, live music, and delightful ambience.

Sharpham Vineyard

SHARPHAM HOUSE. ASHPRINGTON. NR. TOTNES. **Tel: (01803) 732203**

Here in this exquisite woodland setting, with the vines reaching down to the River Dart, you will discover some of the finest wines - and cheeses - in the whole of the U.K.!

Numerous awards for both - many international. Both wines and cheese are made in traditional fashion. Mark Sharman, who runs the vineyard, has been named as one of the three winemakers who will take this art forward into the 21st century. (Decanter Magazine). A lovely place to visit, with delightful walks, wine tastings and the opportunity to taste - and buy - some of the very best.

MEMBER OF THE
SOUTH HAMS FOOD &
DRINK ASSOCIATION

The Elbow Room

NORTH STREET · TOTNES · TELEPHONE: (01803) 863480

The Elbow Room is one of those places you find, and go back to again and again. A 17th century cottage in the old part of Totnes, this is a restaurant which also has accommodation. Open for lunch on Wednesdays and Thursdays and dinner Tuesday to Saturday inclusive. **NOT** Sundays. Examples from the menus include crispy roast duck with orange and cointreau; fillet of English beef with horseradish & mustard or Dart Salmon with range hollandaise. Imaginative starters and desserts plus coffee - and all at reasonable prices. Major cards welcome. A fine restaurant and a delightful place to stay.

Ticklemore Fish

10 TICKLEMORE STREET, TOTNES

Telephone: (01803) 867805

Never mind jokes about tickled trout - you are the one who will be tickled to discover this super shop. Fresh fish straight of the trawlers every day, include all the favourites, including sea bass, fresh crabs, lobsters and scallops. Ticklemore fish also has a selection of frozen and smoked seafoods; sauces and condiments and a pasta/salad bar. Fresh pasta is made ON THE PREMISES every day. There is nothing quite like fresh pasta, and this includes tagliatelle to fusilli, spaghetti and various shells. Wonderful selection, ideal vegetarian fare. They even offer cooking instructions! Simon Osborn and his staff are on hand to advise and assist you in your selection.

The Normandy Arms

BLACKAWTON. TOTNES.
Telephone: (01803) 712316

It is not the easiest place to find, but I can assure you that it is well worth the little extra effort involved! This fine, unspoilt country inn offers an escape from the tedium of daily pressures. With five en suite bedrooms with colour T.V. and all the basic comforts, you can enjoy open fires in winter, Real Ales and good food. The inn was named after the Normandy D-Day landings, and displays interesting military memorabilia from the period. Home-made soup, with granary bread, traditional steak & kidney pie and fresh fish are offered on the snack menu, and there is a fine selection on the a la carte menu including 'Devonish Pork' (escallop of pork fillet, sauteed in butter with cider, mushrooms, onions and double cream), along with chicken, fish and steaks. Location: take the Totnes to Kingsbridge road to Halwell left towards Dartmouth. Turn right at the Forces Tavern. 2 miles to Blackawton.

A UNIQUE CRAFT & VISITOR CENTRE

The Cider Press Centre, once the home of Dartington cider, now gives its name to a unique retail and exhibition centre, showing some of the country's leading craft work. Set in the beautiful Devon countryside, the Centre boasts one of the largest collections of Dartington crystal, plus jewellery and pottery, a fine selection of farm foods, plants and herbs, books, perfumes and toiletries, kitchenware, stationery and prints, and traditional crafts & toys. Spend a delightful day strolling in lovely surroundings, browsing over beautiful things.

DARTINGTON
CIDER PRESS CENTRE

Shinners Bridge, Dartington, Nr. Totnes. Tel: 01803 864171
Opening Times 9.30am - 5.30pm
Monday-Saturday All Year Round

Floyd's Inn *(Sometimes)*

TUCKENHAY. TOTNES. **Telephone: (01803) 732353**

Yes, you will find Keith Floyd pottering about in his own pub from time to time, and it must be said that T.V. celebrity Keith certainly knows how to choose a wonderful inn! On the banks of the River Dart in delightful Tuckenhay, near Totnes, the inn is open 7 days a week - although the restaurant is closed on Sunday evenings and all day Mondays. Booking is essential for the George Restaurant, but there is usually a table available in the Canteen Restaurant. The food is excellent, as you would expect, and in the summer there is a barbecue on the Quay, or classical seafood service with French style 'fruits de mer'. There are bar snacks, but this is not an inn to visit for a ploughman's lunch or sandwich. In Autumn and Winter there are log fires with roast chestnuts, and the winter fare menu includes jugged hare and pheasant. Throughout the year both restaurants feature Keith Floyd's international dishes.

There are three simply superb 'en suite' rooms. They are expensive, but the sheer luxury, decor and ambience of staying here ensures the rationale of your extravagance! A sauna, sunbed and snooker room complete the picture of what you may expect, and manager Mike Atkinson is dedicated to preserving the quality and service for which this inn is famed.

The inn can also be reached by boat from Totnes and Dartmouth, and there are moorings on the Quayside. Chef Christophe Vincent is chef de cuisine and some of his creations are simply brilliant. Try the Lobster souffle with vodka sauce, or noisette of Roe Deer with game sauce, red cabbage and glazed chestnuts. Most major credit cards are welcome.

DARTMOUTH

Dartmouth is 13 miles from Totnes and in high season visitors are advised to make full use of the park and ride facility well sign-posted on the outskirts of the town. Parking alongside the embankment and in the central car park is soon taken and much of Dartmouth, like Totnes, is easily explored on foot. Dartmouth Castle can be reached via a road sign-posted around the back of Dartmouth without having actually to pass through the town. Dartmouth Pottery can be reached the same way.

The river Dart has a magic no other river can offer and has been described as the English Rhine with the Anchor Stone replacing the Lorelei Rock. However the Dart is English of the English, and along its bank, in its meadows and among the buildings great events and people in our history are enshrined in memory. To Devonians it is not the River Dart, just 'Dart'. Dartmouth itself is dramatically situated, like many Devon towns, built on the side of a steep, wooded valley overlooking the river. Queen Victoria wrote of it in her diary - "20th August 1846. It was thought best to give up Lynmouth and put in at that beautiful Dartmouth, and we accordingly did so in pouring rain, the deck swimming with water, and all of us with umbrellas ... not withstanding the rain, this place is lovely with its wooded rocks and castles at the entrance ..." She was of course referring to the twin castles which guard the entrance to the river for it has always been a defensive port; Warfleet Creek has sheltered numerous assembled fleets of warships; during the fear of French invasion in 1388 the people of Dartmouth were building a small fortress at the entrance to the Dart when John Hawley was mayor - the man who Chaucer, whilst visiting the town in 1373, probably used as a model for the character of Schipman or Shipman in Canterbury Tales.

There are some remains of this fortalice or small fortress in the shape of a curtain wall and the ruin of a tower close to the present car park below the hillside; however once the influence and interest of Hawley had gone, the old castle site was abandoned, a castle was built later within the ruins, but again deserted in 1539. During the 15th century a form of defence was maintained by stretching a chain across the harbour mouth known as 'Jawbones'. This was said to be kept 'in good repair, carried across by small boats called cobles, six in number being adequate for the job, the chain fixed into a hole in the cliff near Godmerock'. It was not until 1481 there is any record of the construction

The Inner Harbour.

Bayard's Cove.

Looking across to Kingswear.

The Lower Ferry.

of the castle which remains today. From the records of accounts dated 1488-95 weapons were purchased with ample supplies of powder and shot, four watchmen were stationed permanently. The work on the companion castle on the Kingswear side was begun in 1491, similar in style to the square tower of Dartmouth, but by the 1620s this also was abandoned and became a ruin. In 1855 Charles Seale-Hayne, a rich merchant who dominated the life of Dartmouth during part of the 18th and 19th centuries, brought it back into use as a summer residence. Above Dartmouth castle stands Gallants Bower, a good example of fortifications at the time of the Civil War.

After this time the defence of Dartmouth was maintained only with the idea of an attack from the sea. It was kept on a war footing during the Dutch wars, and over the next few years there were bursts of activity during times of war, with long periods of neglect and decay in peace time.

During the First World War two 4.7 Quick Fire guns from the Imperial Workshops in Japan were mounted, and then removed in 1937.

In 1940 the Castle was again made ready for action, the two guns restored in a pillarbox with crenellations as camouflage. In 1955 what remained was put into guardianship as an Ancient Monument and since 1983 has been in the care of the Heritage Trust.

Within the old castle stands St. Petrox Church built in memory of a Celtic Saint who died in 594, mentioned as early as 1192 it was rebuilt in the 17th century with a small western tower, the churchyard full of many typical westcountry slate memorials. Occasional weddings, christenings and funerals still take place and on a summer evening the bells still sound sweetly across the water to the town.

Dartmouth is built on terraces, originally two fishing hamlets lying either side of a creek which became a millpond along the present course of the Victoria Road. The first houses clung to the hillside above the tide line, and some of the streets face a slope with a sudden flight of steps so that first floor windows gaze into the attics of their opposite numbers; some seem to hang above the water, as the historian Prince wrote - "in rows like galley pots in an apothecary's shop" Dartmouth really came into its own after the Norman Conquest and down the years it has been the assembly port for the departure of vessels to do battle in every corner of the world.

From here sailed the ships of the Second Crusade, boats on the first of the great East Indiamen, and on D-Day some 480 vessels bound for the Normandy beaches.

But it was the voyages to Newfoundland that brought most prosperity when the town contributed as many ships to this new fishing ground as most other major ports. A fleet would sail away for the fishing grounds early in the season carrying the dried fish back to the European markets to trade for cargoes of fruit and wine, as well as the cloth made in the fulling mills of the countryside of Devon, which was world famous.

The results of these merchants' riches can be seen in the beautiful buildings, the churches and houses and the quay which is the pride and centre of the town and Bayard's Cove, sometimes known as Bearcove, with its cobbled courtyard facing onto the river from whence the Pilgrim Fathers aboard the 'Mayflower' and 'Speedwell' sailed on 20th August 1620. Having sailed from Southampton they put into Dartmouth for repairs to the Speedwell, which was leaking. With the repairs completed they both left the harbour to continue their journey only once again to turn back when the Speedwell sprang another leak. This time they returned to Plymouth and it was just the 'Mayflower' which left Plymouth on the 16th September, reaching America safely on November 21st 1620. From here too sailed the flower of Richard Coeur de Lion's Crusade. As you stand here, caught in a time warp, you can imagine the great ships coming round from ports like Plymouth, rowed by a hundred oarsman, carrying men and horses for the crusades; the sound of trumpets on the breeze, the neighing of horses huddled in the stern.

In 1346 it is said Dartmouth sent more ships to the siege of Calais than any other town in England save Fowey and Yarmouth. Thirty years later the French got their own back by setting Dartmouth on fire.

In this atmosphere of the past the area probably looks much as it did in the 14th century, the buildings being much older than the cobbles and paving bricks which were laid in 1665, the year before the Great Fire of London. The buildings themselves have names which are part of history itself - Agincourt House, Morocco House with its ornamental iron balcony and beautiful door, the Customs House dated 1739 which has a long room with a perfect plastered ceiling.

The oldest part of this area is the Bulwark, Bayard's Cove Fort, built in 1509-10 to protect the harbour, but said to be obsolete before the mortar was dry due to bad design for the embrasures have an inward splay instead of outward, as the Home Guard found to their cost when in 1940 they tried to adapt it as a strong point of defence. In 1937 it is mentioned as the 'New Castle' in a corporation lease and Leland in 1553-54 described it as "A fair bulwark, built of late". Irregular of plan with thick walls pierced by eleven gunports with a wall walk and parapet above, it covers the narrowest part of the channel at the entrance to Dartmouth Harbour and has been in the care of English Heritage since 1984.

From this harbour in the years 1871 - 1891 The Cape and Natal Steamship Co. picked up mail and passengers and there was a regular steamship service to South Africa and Australia.

Dartmouth also served as a bunkering port, steamships needed refuelling points and by 1868 coal hulks were moored in mid-stream, filled from the old sailing colliers from Wales and the shipping boom brought vessels from all over the world to Dartmouth. A famous local boat was the Mew built in 1905 for the Great Western Railway. She operated between Kingswear station and 'Dartmouth Station', a building in the exact style of the standard railway station with booking office and waiting room. Passengers bought their tickets here, went aboard the Mew and sailed across to Kingswear where they picked up the train. The popular holiday line of the Paignton and Dartmouth Steam Railway now has steam trains running for seven miles in Great Western tradition along the spectacular coast to Churston and through the wooded slopes bordering the Dart estuary before eventually returning to Kingswear. As for the Mew, she went to Dunkirk during the Second World War and returned safely, later to rescue a boat called the Mistral which was drifting towards the rocks between Bayard's Cove and Warfleet.

A naval captain stationed here during the war wrote of his memories when engaged in E boat patrols in Lyme Bay and Start Point ... "We would spend all night at sea and return to our base ship in early morning anchored in the centre of the harbour next to a small boat run by Naval Intelligence. They had two gunboats in which they ferried agents across the channel to occupied France, bringing back other agents for a rest. Before D-Day the whole harbour changed dramatically, teeming with landing craft of every shape and size, practising for the D-Day landings. At this time in the war, 1943, there was nothing afloat in the Channel except ourselves, E boats and an occasional small convoy of merchant ships hugging the British coast - rather different from today!"

Different indeed from the teeming waterfront with its ever changing kaleidoscope of boats of every size and type. Two ferries sail across from shore to shore, the lower one to Kingswear, probably in existence long before it was first referred to in 1365. The higher ferry was opened in 1832 when the new road to Brixham was built.

Just above the higher ferry stands the Dart Marina boasting a collection of yachts which a year's lottery prizes would hardly buy.

The most outstanding building in the town is the Britannia Royal Naval College, first established in wooden hulled warships, the Britannia and Hindustan, moored off Sandquay. Britannia was brought from Portland in 1863 and the Hindustan in 1864; the shore buildings designed by Sir Aston Webb were built between 1899 and 1905. It was there our present Queen first met the man she was to marry, during a royal visit when Prince Philip was a cadet at the College. Here too King George VI, Prince Charles and Prince Andrew started their service careers. During the war there were heavy raids on Dartmouth in 1942 and 1943 when some bombs hit the College, but fortunately it was on the day before the cadets were due to return from holiday.

Another fascinating area of the town is the Butterwalk said to be the finest remaining example of 17th century Devonian style domestic architecture, built in 1635, and so called because the farmers' wives could sell their produce in the shade of its colonnade. The half timbered buildings house galleries, chandleries, delicatessens, specialist gift shops, handicrafts etc. On Saturday 13th February 1943 the Butterwalk was hit by bombs when all the windows were blown out and the pillars buckled. Repairs where completed in 1953 and the Butterwalk was opened again in 1954. The Dartmouth Museum is based in one of the 17th century Merchants' houses with an emphasis on matters maritime, a superb display of model ships and paintings.

The Henley Museum holds a unique collection of every day Victorian possessions once belonging to the Dartmouth sage, William Henley, 1860 to 1919. These include a microscope and slides, fossils, photographs and a reconstruction of his living room. He was apprenticed to his father in ironmongery and a tinsmith. He had no education after the age of 12, but taught himself everything from languages to botany, and natural sciences; he was a gifted painter and etcher. This collection is a unique record of vanished Dartmouth, and the Museum is open from Easter to October.

In 1663 Thomas Newcomen invented the atmospheric steam engine which heralded the industrial revolution, and was much used in the mines. One of the few remaining pumping engines is exhibited in the Newcomen Engine House and this particular engine once worked in Griff Colliery and also at the Coventry Canal. Entrance to the Engine house is gained from the Tourist

Information Centre in Royal Avenue Gardens. The gardens, with bandstand, are found between the car park and inner harbour.

Dartmouth is a network of narrow streets and unusual buildings with a variety of shops offering everything from books, pottery, food, to shoes and jewellery. In summer it is a mass of flowers for it is an annual entrant in the Britain in Bloom competition and at the end of August the Regatta takes place, the highlight of the season as it has been for the last 150 years. The inner harbour is tidal with a control at the entrance, but when the tide is high the boats seem to be floating in the street. Opposite stands the Royal Castle Hotel with a ghost coach that haunts the hall. The date over the door is 1639 but probably the first building on this site was much older. As regards the ghost, legend has it that Princess Mary of Orange didn't like travelling by sea and sailed for England, landing at Dartmouth while the fine weather held without waiting for her husband William who intended to follow immediately with his army. However bad weather made him land at Brixham instead. He sent a horseman to Dartmouth to tell his wife and bid her be ready for the coach that was coming to bring her and her ladies to join him. It arrived hot on the heels of the messenger at 2 am, and still does so. What was once the yard is now the hall and many people have heard the rumble of wheels, the clatter of hooves and coach doors banging. No one can explain why this haunting takes place or when it will occur.

It is not easy to tear oneself away from Dartmouth and mention must be made of the steep flight of steps in Higher Street which lead up to the Cherub pub. A plaque outside states it is the oldest surviving mediaeval house in Dartmouth, believed to have been built in or about 1380 and described thus - "It is a wooden framed house of a townsman and has two very unusual two-light windows on the first floor of a type not previously seen."

Both visitors and locals are spoiled for choice among the cafes, restaurants, inns and other eating places which provide the cream of Devon food - literally. Fish and shellfish are locally caught, meat, poultry, fruit and vegetables - even the real ale, cider and wines are all local produce. If you wish to explore a little way beyond the town, five miles away is Woodlands Leisure Park with 60 acres of indoor and outdoor fun with play zones, slides, animals, a honey farm and waterfowl all in a beautiful wooded valley in Blackawton on the A 3122. For the grown ups nearby is the Dartmouth Golf and Country Club, a championship course with luxurious clubhouse - both Societies and visitors are welcome on payment of green fees. Along the waterfront in Dartmouth itself are seats where one can sit and watch the world go by, mostly waterborne, and here is a wide choice of river cruises run by both companies and individuals offering trips up the Dart, something which really is part of the history of the town. The journey lasts just over an hour as the story of life along the banks unfolds, a history lesson in itself.

The first curiosity on the trip is the Anchor Stone, a marker warns river users of its presence. History has it that Sir Walter Raleigh sought refuge here when he wanted a quiet smoke. It has also been called the Scold Stone because the men of Dittisham (sometimes pronounced Ditsam) who lived on the nearby bank of the river were said to put their unruly wives here until they calmed down. During the war a hospital ship was moored nearby. The village is famous for its Dittisham plums which grow nowhere else, said to have been dumped here from a German cargo boat - the German for plum is plumen so sometimes they are known as ploughmen. On the opposite bank is Greenway Quay, now with only a ferry for foot passengers. Once there was a ferry for cattle, sheep and cows for Churston fatstock market, but more often than not the animals ended up in the river. A later one for cars in the form of a pontoon was rowed with paddles. In 1964 a motor boat powered by water jets was introduced to tow the pontoon, but it didn't pay and was abandoned. Here also the Dimblebys of television fame have a house. There is a Sailing School with tuition and hire facilities for beginners and advanced pupils in Wayfarer sailing dinghies.

At Greenway John and Humphrey Gilbert had their childhood home and Agatha Christie's modern house looked across to Dittisham. At Galmpton Creek the river suddenly becomes almost two miles wide and here the skeletons of old wrecks give it a rather desolate feeling. Motor Torpedo Boats were built here during the war and deep in the woods was a stone cellar where smugglers once hid their brandy and tobacco on moonless nights, sacking covering the donkeys' hooves so they made no sound. There are still small quays at the river's edge where some of the residents launch their boats, at one time cider in hogsheads was brought to the quays when the tide was high to load on to the barges. Several mansions are hidden in the woods - Sandridge House built in 1805 to the design of John Nash of Regent Street fame. John Davis the navigator was born nearby at Sandridge Barton. He was the 16th century navigator who discovered the Davis straits whilst looking for the north west passage. It is said 'men left their firesides to sail with him on the three voyages he made to the Arctic'.

Stoke Gabriel is a pretty sprawling village with a mill pool and waterfront, its chief claim to fame stands in the churchyard, a yew tree said to be the oldest in England, possibly having stood here since the Norman Conquest.

Another piece of fascinating history concerns the house now called Maisonette. It stands at the top of a steep lane leading down to Duncannon Creek. At one time it was known as Stoke Gabriel House, built for a mistress of George IV who came all the way from Brighton by post chaise to visit his love. At one time Captain James RN lived there. He had been the commander of the old Britannia training ship. Pleasure boats used to stop here for people to come ashore either to climb the hill and see the view, or to be ferried across to Ashprington. Opposite Stoke Gabriel is an inlet to Bow Creek fed by the Harbourne and Wash. At the top stands Tuckenhay, during the 19th century a busy little port with paper and corn mills, and now famous for its Floyds Inn, owned by television chef Keith Floyd.

The river itself now makes an 'S' bend with two promentaries, on the western one stands Sharpham House. It has had many distinguished residents including the Durants and the Bastards. The estate now has a vineyard and creamery making fine English wine and cheeses.

Now comes the narrowest and least interesting part of the river with flat and featureless countryside. The only object of interest is Parker's Barn where, in the days when Totnes sent members to Parliament, much skulduggery took place over getting them elected, many people were offered large sums of money to vote, or not to vote, for a particular candidate; if this failed other methods were used. 'Mr Parker' was plied with strong drink and when he passed out put in the barn and the door locked until the voting was over.

As Totnes comes into light, the deep, still water seems bottomless and gazing down one thinks of the reflections of the past, of thousands of people who have passed up and down this river - Pheonicians, Romans, Normans, Saxons and Dutch, all with their different means of propulsion - the river up which it is said the Roman General Brutus took five days to negotiate coming at last to Toto Naise.

The · Red · Lion · Inn

Dittisham · Dartmouth · Devon · TQ6 0ES
Telephone/Fax: (01803) 722235

Set in a village on the beautiful Dart Estuary, the Red Lion Inn is a Free House, open all year. A superb English country inn with a renowned restaurant and lovely accommodation. Five bedrooms, all en suite with colour television, hairdryers etc., and excellent facilities for functions and weddings. Log fires, wonderful views, Real Ales and menus to make your mouth water !
Very reasonable prices .This inn is one of Woody's favourites. Booking in advance is recommended if you wish to dine here.

Resident Hosts; Stephen & Margaret Winter

MEMBER OF THE
SOUTH HAMS FOOD &
DRINK ASSOCIATION

49

LANGWORTHY'S
HOME MADE ICE CREAM & FUDGE

30 LOWER STREET. DARTMOUTH. S. DEVON.
Telephone: (01803) 832157

The Good Intent is the home of Devon's finest home-made dairy ice cream, and is located opposite the Lower Ferry in Dartmouth. Dairy ice cream has been produced here since before the war, but recipes have changed and Langworthys now offer more than 20 flavours using the finest fresh fruit and other natural ingredients. We also make our own ice cream cakes, fruit ices & delicious fudge.

MEMBER OF THE
SOUTH HAMS FOOD &
DRINK ASSOCIATION

HOUSE OF HAWKINS
10 FOSS STREET. DARTMOUTH. DEVON.
Telephone: (01803) 833845

Established over 75 years ago, the House of Hawkins is a family run fine menswear shop situated in Dartmouth's beautiful Foss Street. Here is real quality, and leading makes like Crombie, John G. Hardy, Magee and Odermark are stocked, together with many other quality names. Some of the largest stocks of Viyella and Clydella to be found in the Westcountry are offered together with continental makes such as Seidensticker and Melka, with Dexter, Church and Grenson shoes, and Jaeger knitwear.

THE CUTTER'S BUNCH

33 LOWER STREET. DARTMOUTH. DEVON. **Tel: (01803) 832882**

The Cutter's Bunch is an evening restaurant - and one of the very best. Open from 7.00 p.m. *(NOT Wednesdays)* it is located just near the lower ferry. Imaginative menus change from day to day, featuring the very best of local fish and seafood and other fine fare. Local lobster with calvados cream sauce; roast guinea hen in madeira sauce; Thai seafood pot *(scallops, squid, mussels and giant prawns cooked Thai fashion)*, or venison with honey and red wine. Owners Nick Crosley and Jo Walters-Symons spend each day preparing what Woody can only describe as their culinary magic for the evening. Prior notice needed for vegetarian meals. Quite superb!

The EXCHANGE RESTAURANT

5 HIGHER STREET · DARTMOUTH · DEVON   **Tel: (01803) 832022**

This outstanding restaurant is owned and run by chef/proprietor David Hawke. The Exchange dates from 1352 and is a fine example of period architecture, and is also a former Mayor's residence. Specialities prepared from local produce and seafoods. The restaurant opens at 10.30 am for coffee; lunch from 12 noon to 2.30 pm; dinner 7.00 pm to 10.00 pm. Prices are reasonable. Most imaginative menus. Starters include mushrooms with cumin; blackbean cakes with roasted red pepper coulis and crabmeat Newburg. Main courses vary from lambs liver braised with gin and avocado to sirloin steak with rum, peppercorn and cream sauce! Menus change to take advantage of the best of the day's catch … or the season's fare.

THE ROYAL CASTLE HOTEL

THE QUAY. DARTMOUTH. DEVON. TQ6 9PS   **Telephone: (01803) 833033**

Step into history, an ideal venue at anytime of the year. Unique 17th century coaching hostelry combines the finest traditions of English Innkeeping with today's comforts. 25 luxuriously appointed en suite bedrooms are individually decorated and furnished, many with 4 poster or brass beds, fine antiques and jacuzzi. Elegant restaurant overlooks the estuary and specialises in select regional produce, locally caught seafood and fine wines. 2 bars serve choice meals, ales and wines, and open log fires burn during cooler months.

MEMBER OF THE
SOUTH HAMS FOOD &
DRINK ASSOCIATION

The Ferry Boat

DITTISHAM. NR. DARTMOUTH. DEVON. **Tel: 01803 722368**

"One of the finest views from any bar in the country" said the Daily Telegraph. This 18th century inn stands so close to the river that at low tide the beach is part of the car park. The food, prepared by owner Ann Beney, is first class, and when I was there on a 'theme evening' French style, the food earned her an enthusiastic round of applause. In winter a theme evening is held every month. Seafood, homemade pizzas, pasta dishes, ploughmans' lunches and daily specials of appetising variety and excellent crab sandwiches. There are Real Ales and a lovely relaxed 'nautical' atmosphere about the place.

Children under 14 are not permitted. Arrive by boat if you can ..... otherwise by car, follow signs to the passenger ferry.

Billy Budd's LICENSED BISTRO

7 FOSS STREET. DARTMOUTH. DEVON.
Telephone: (01803) 833845

Here, in Dartmouth's lovely Foss Street, is a true bistro! Full of character, with wooden tables, chairs and benches, Billy Budds exudes relaxed comfort and informality; an atmosphere in which to enjoy the pleasures of country-style hospitality, home-fare, and fine - but not expensive - wines. Pasta and omelettes and similar light fare at lunchtime; moules mariniere, crevettes with garlic dip, noisettes of lamb with ratatouille, supreme of chicken and fillet of beef au poivre are examples from the evening menus. Try the fresh roast duck with plum sauce or the grilled John Dory maitre 'D if you want a special treat! Reasonable prices, but there is a minimum charge of £10.95. per person in the evening. In Woody's opinion this is real value for money.

Proprietors: KEITH & LYNNE

GEORGE & DRAGON

MAYORS AVENUE. DARTMOUTH. **Telephone: (01803) 832325**

A stone's throw from the Quay in Dartmouth, The George & Dragon is very much a part of the Dartmouth scene. A super beer garden, part canopy-covered, provides a fine 'al fresco' setting where you can sit with your drink - and food - and watch the passing scene. Open all day, every day in summer, here you will find Real Ales and home-cooked food. Steak and mushroom pie; a variety of curries and veggie dishes vie with specials of the day such as 'Fillet George' - a dish you MUST try consisting of fillet steak strips with courgettes, mushrooms, garlic and herbs! Fresh fish every day, and all-inclusive children's menu. Limited accommodation.

The Hungry Horse Restaurant

OLD ROAD. HARBERTONFORD. DEVON.
Telephone: (01803) 732441

MEMBER OF THE
SOUTH HAMS FOOD &
DRINK ASSOCIATION

This true Devon cottage restaurant can be found in the village of Harbertonford on the main Totnes to Kingsbridge road. Open Tuesday to Saturday from 7 pm to 10.30 pm (last orders) the Hungry Horse is also open for lunch during the summer. In a lovely setting, overlooking the river, they specialise in quality local produce such as sea bass, fresh mussels (with shallots, garlic, white wine and cream!) and other delights of forest, field, river and ocean.

Dishes such as the rillettes of duck and smoked pork with Port served with toast have become something of a legend here, and the warm relaxed atmosphere , fine wine list and ever varying selection will appeal to all tastes. Visa/Mastercard welcome. Booking is advisable.

The Carved Angel

2 SOUTH EMBANKMENT · DARTMOUTH
Telephone: (01803) 832465

Internationally famous, Dartmouth's Carved Angel restaurant has received accolades from all the major guides and food writers. Open for lunch *(Tuesday to Sunday)* and dinner *(Tuesday to Saturday)*, the restaurant is open all year, except in January and early February. There is insufficient space to do justice to the superb menus, but be assured that the reputation of the Carved Angel is enough of a guarantee of excellence. Fixed menu prices; No credit cards accepted. (Lunch £24+ per person; dinner £40+)

START BAY

The piece of coastline running from Dartmouth to Wembury is some of the most beautiful in England; it is also the backdrop to more wrecks, piracy and smuggling - the latter still in full swing - perhaps with more lethal contraband than when it was 'Brandy for the Parson, and 'baccy for the clerk.' Start Bay runs from the mouth of the Dart estuary to Start Point. The first village beyond the estuary is Stoke Fleming. Perhaps difficult to believe, but at the time of the Domesday Book (1084) it was bigger and more important than Dartmouth. Although Dartmouth is now considerably larger, Stoke Fleming has actually grown in size unlike some villages which are away from the major towns and have declined through lack of work for the young who have had to go further afield to earn a living. The church of St. Peter stands on a hill and was said to be built as a marker for ships entering the Dart. George Parker Bidder, the famous 'Calculating Boy' who 'amused' even Queen Victoria with his amazing knowledge and is also remembered for his amazing engineering knowledge put into practice throughout Europe's railway projects, bought a house in Stoke Fleming and is buried in the churchyard here. Beyond here is one of the most popular beaches in the area known as Blackpool Sands, a wood lined cove comparable with the

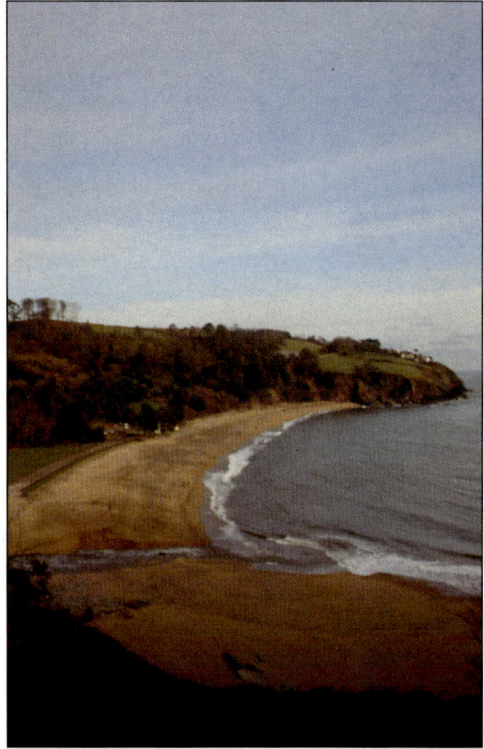

Blackpool Sands.

Mediterranean beaches - hardly to be compared with its Northern namesake! It is an idyllic spot with its clear water and fine shingle and caters well for the family day out with ample parking, food takeaways, shop, toilets, an ice cream stall and other amenities. The water is deep for the keen swimmer and there are rock pools for the children - be warned though, dogs are not welcome. The beach took a battering with the storm that swept this area in 1990 when part of the road collapsed and took many months to restore. In 1869 the tide and wind removed the sand from the south western end of the beach to the clay beneath, some tree stumps emerged which proved it and had been a submerged forest. In 1404 there was a bloody attack here by the Bretons led by Du Chatel, who was killed and many people say they feel some kind of atmosphere here. Henry IV ordered a Te Deum to be sung in Westminster Abbey as a result of the victory. This beach in company with Slapton, Torcross and Bantham are Tidy Britain Group Rural Beach Award winners with the highest standard of bathing water quality.

The 'line'.

Strete like Stoke Fleming, stands a little aloof on a hill from which are the most beautiful views over real South Hams countryside. Below can be seen Slapton Sands, oddly named for a shingle beach, where the road runs at sea level for one and a half miles beside a long stretch of shingle barrier. This is 'The Line' and to the north landward side of the road is Slapton Ley Nature Reserve. Slapton Ley is the freshwater lake enclosed behind the shingle bank. A Site of Special Scientific Interest and National Nature Reserve, it provides a unique habitat for resident and migrating birds. At the Torcross end of the Ley look out for an unusual road-sign, warning that here, birds have priority. Nearby, you will find they congregate, the resident ducks looking for food, delighting young and old visitors alike. The information board will help you with identification.

The Ley is owned and managed by the Herbert Whitley Trust, owners of Paignton Zoo and Botanical Gardens. They have worked hard to protect the site, and have created an open nature trail round the Ley. They run the Slapton Field Centre in the nearby village, where much study of the amazing wildlife of the area is undertaken, ranging from fresh and sea water birds, (resident and visiting), flowers and reeds to small mammals and lichens. Geologists consider the shingle bank to have stabilized 3,000 years ago and the lake to be at least 1,000 years old. It is fed by two streams, the Gara and the Start. It is interesting that quite different animals, birds and plants occur either side of this protective shingle bank; to the seaward side lies Start Bay. Its marine life once ensured a good living to the fishermen of Hallsands, Beesands and Torcross in the catching of crabs and lobsters. The shore supports a garden of wild flowers such as the yellow horned poppy, sea radish,

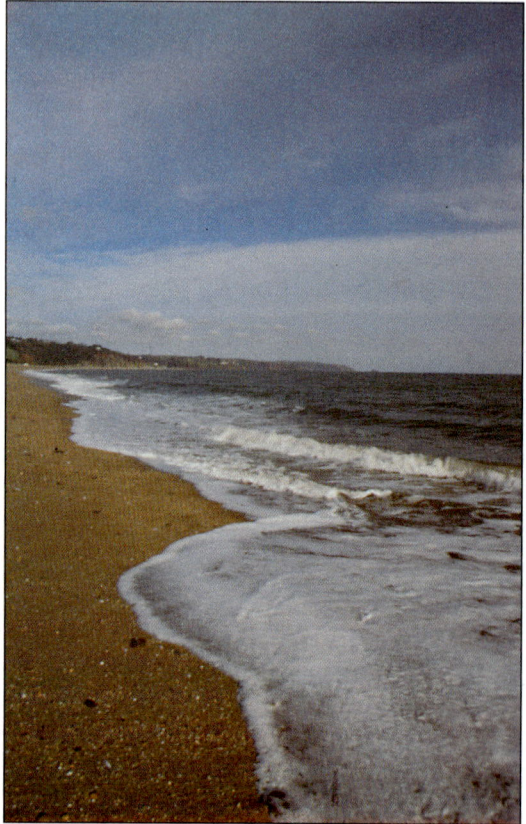
Slapton beach and Start Bay.

sea carrot, rest harrow and many more. On the landward side grow gorse and brambles, the latter producing huge juicy berries. Among the many other flowers is vipers bluegloss.

The water is not very deep and much of the reed here was once harvested for roofing thatch. The woods behind were planted early in the 19th century to provide timber for the Royal Navy.

Behind the Ley and the woods is the village of Slapton, also mentioned in Domesday, most likely settled by the Iron Age people who built a fort here. The Anglo Saxons named it Sladona - a slippery place. In 1372 Sir Guy de

Brien founded a chantry, the ruins of which can be seen near the pub. The local people in bygone days were not averse to supplementing their living by looting wrecked ships of which there were hundreds, including the Navis Dei wrecked on Slapton Sands in 1302.

In 1864 a bridge and turnpike were built along the line of the old packhorse track from Torcross to Strete, and a coach service ran from Kingsbridge to Dartmouth until the First World War. This meant a new lease of life for a group of buildings on 'The Line', formerly known as Slapton Cellars which became the Sands Hotel, soon to change its name to the Royal Sands Hotel after a visit from the young King Edward VII when at Dartmouth College.

Slapton Ley.

Of course the most memorable time in the whole history of the life of Slapton, Sherford, Blackawton and all the other villages in this area, was the evacuation in 1943 in preparation for the landings by the US Forces on the Normandy beaches on D-Day, code named 'Exercise Tiger'. An area in the form of a triangular wedge from the coast to the hillside village of Blackawton which was its apex. This involved seven parishes, 180 farms, 750 families - all told about 3,000 people being affected. Perhaps it was a foretaste of what was to come when the Royal Sands Hotel abruptly ended its lifespan when 'Pincher' Luscombe, a sheepdog from Slapton, strayed into the closed area chasing a rabbit under the wire round the hotel causing land mines to explode. Many more explosions were to shake the area.

Slapton Village.

The villagers were told of this evacuation at a meeting in the village hall at

Slapton on 13th November, 1943 when the people were told they had to clear the whole area by 20th December. The official British Government Statement ran thus:

"We are calling on the people as their War sacrifice to give up their homes and land temporarily for the quartering and second front training of the American soldiers."

The weather was dank and dreary, there was a 'flu epidemic and many of the inhabitants were elderly and had never even left the parish in which they lived, many families had remained in the same house for generations. Somehow they had to move their cattle, even the turnips in the ground. Corn had to be threshed, no combine harvesters in those days. The delicate fabric of many of the old churches caused great concern and had to be preserved in the best way possible, screens removed, silver taken away and the rest of the building sandbagged. A complete hush descended on the area, forlorn villages with cottages and houses whose windows were closed and sightless. No birds sang, only rats lived on and ate the putty from the windows. Many books about the evacuation and American occupation have been written and can be purchased locally.

Eventually D-Day came and went. People returned to their homes and to ruined,potholed fields, choked with nettles and brambles. It took nearly ten years to right it. Some people never returned, there was death and suicide and

The Sherman Tank raised from the seabed during 1984.

yet the secret was so well kept that no one in the rest of England had an inkling of what had happened. All that remains as a reminder of those dark days is a memorial where the Sands Hotel once stood, erected by the Americans as a gesture of thanks to the villagers, and at Torcross car park a Sherman tank which was raised from the sea-bed in 1984. Many American troops were killed when a convoy of landing craft they were using for an exercise was attacked by German 'E' boats (torpedo boats), sinking two of the craft and crippling others. Today it is difficult to believe the havoc that took place as you look out at the calm sea and the gaily painted white walled cottages, some thatched, some with slated roofs. One thing is certain you will be spoilt for choice when it comes to eating and drinking, every pub and restaurant offers home cooked food, fresh fish straight from the sea, in fact some of the plaice put before you appears to be a junior edition of Jaws so big are they. Seafood is of course a speciality, including fresh crabs and prawns, all of which can be washed down with local cider and beer, and in summer eaten outside close to the sea, or indoors by a roaring log fire during winter. One of the local inns won the Finest Fish Award in the Good Pub Guide and customers regularly come from as far afield as Exeter to sample it.

Torcross village was the first of two old coastal settlements built dangerously close to the sea, taking its name from the great rock which dominates the southern end of the beach. The whereabouts of the cross is not known, perhaps it once stood on the summit of the rock as a mark for shipping.

Like its neighbours of Beesands and Hallsands, Torcross was well known in the 19th century for its crabs, huge supplies being sent to London daily. The seafront was devastated in 1951 when a large section of the old promenade was undermined by the sea, a massive concrete cavity wall was built at the southern end of the village where the damage was worst, and a cheaper construction at the northern end. The locals had warned the council about this and in January 1979 it did indeed prove to be totally inadequate when the sea broke through the defences causing enormous damage to sea front properties said to amount to £1/2 million. Laurie Emberson who was living in the village, wrote an account of the storm 'The Torcross Disaster', a story of complete dedication by one man to save his village by forcing the authorities to build an adequate defence against the sea. His description of the night of the storm is brilliant, and it is almost impossible to believe, as you stand looking at the tranquil sea on a warm summer afternoon, the devastation that was caused. Now you can see the completed wall for which he fought.

Beesands was once a thriving fishing village, now with only a vestige of fishing left, but for the summer visitor an idyllic place to sit on the beach in the lee of the great boulders put there to protect the village against winds and tide. The local inn has pictures of the storms which hit the village just as it did Torcross in January 1979 when the sea went over the roofs of the cottages. Many of these are holiday homes and empty in the winter months. Once you could see rows of boats, nets, floats, barrels and crab and lobster pots, all alas no more. The local fishermen will tell you the decline in fishing is due to many factors - the high price of tackle, dwindling markets, and the attraction to younger men of easier and less dangerous work in town. There is too, a mysterious departure of fish from local waters - in fact the amount off the Skerries Bank today is roughly one sixth of what it was 50 years ago. Fish change their habits for no reason, depriving a whole section of the community of their livelihood. But even more tragic happenings can destroy a fishing village - look at what is left of Hallsands.

The village the sea took - it is not certain when Hallsands as an actual village began. The title deeds of the London Inn were dated 1780, it must have been thriving by then. Why the fishermen chose this narrow rock ledge is also not known, there was no reliable supply of drinking water which had to be brought from Lamacraft Farm up the valley, the only access to the village was down the steep trackway from the valley. By 1850 there were 37 houses and a population of 128, most of them men who had other trades apart from fishing. A tailor, carpenter, blacksmith etc so the village was completely self contained. Crab pots were woven from osiers grown in the valley, seine netting was carried out when a boat was rowed round a shoal of fish, most likely mullet, and encircled it with the net, both ends of which were held on the shore. Even the

Hallsands.

women and Newfoundland dogs helped to haul on the ropes, in fact the women played a large part in the whole process, often carrying their men on their backs to the boats so they should not spend the day fishing in wet clothing.

Houses were built by being dovetailed into the angle of rock between beach and cliff, the latter being one wall of the house. Some were thatched, others had slate roofs. The first houses on the seaward side were built on solid rock, but when these ran out, others were built across the sand-filled gullies. A narrow road ran in front of the houses, the whole village was not more than 40ft wide, and protected by a bank of shingle 90 feet wide.

There was a grocer's shop, post office and a Seamen's Mission where lectures and concerts were held. The London Inn was visited by local tourists who came in pleasure steamers from Torquay to drink in the pub with the local fishermen.

In 1894 plans were made to extend Devonport dockyard. Many tonnes of broken stone and shingle were needed. In Start Bay lay the shingle of ideal quality, easy, and cheap to extract. In April 1897 dredging began. Every day 1,600 tonnes of shingle were removed. The whole shape and angle of the beach were altered. The contractor moved his dredgers nearer the village, he believed the holes made would be filled by the tide. By now the villagers were deeply disturbed and asked their Member of Parliament Colonel Mildmay, later Lord Mildmay of Flete, to intervene. In June 1897 a Board of Trade inspector held an enquiry, the contractor won his case. For a short time dredgers and villagers kept an uneasy truce. In the autumn of 1900 the beach levels fell dramatically, no new shingle was coming into the bay. That winter properties on the seaward side began to collapse. Colonel Mildmay again protested and in 1901 the Board of Trade sent an inspector who agreed the position was bad and might get worse. In early January 1902 the dredging licence was cancelled.

Of course it was too late. Fresh storms again altered the level of the beach. Compensation was offered to those who had lost their homes. Masonry blocks were made into a sea wall. Some amount of tranquillity returned to the village. Mr Prettejohn who kept both the Inn and was a fisherman, was one of the first to see the coming danger and in 1904 he moved his family to a house further up the cliff.

The village settled down to some extent, preferring to put up with intermittent flooding rather than leave their homes.

On 26th January, 1917 the storm came which finally overwhelmed the village. The fishermen were expecting an easterly gale, high tide was 10 pm, they hauled their boats up on the beach. The sea broke over the walls, sucked the gravel away and the houses simply collapsed and were battered to pieces by the shingle hurled at them. By midnight four houses were totally demolished.

None actually survived intact. The villagers could not escape in either direction. By dawn the only house still in any way inhabitable was the Prettejohns', the rest were irreparably damaged. The miracle was that no one was killed. In describing the scene Elizabeth Prettejohn said "The sea was full of furniture." Mrs Lamble spoke of her experiences, she was just seventeen years of age and had come home from service where she worked in Salcombe. Her father came up from the beach to his house lit by candles. He went into the scullery to wash his hands for supper. "As he did so the walls caved in and fell down, the sea came down the chimney." The villagers were homeless and had to fend for themselves. Some went to relatives, five of the men shared a hayloft, some took to living in the ruins during the summer months. Eventually money was raised and in 1924 a few cottages were built nearby named Fordworth after Hansford Worth and Mr Ford who had done much for the plight of the villagers. Elizabeth Prettejohn alone went on living in the end house of Hallsands with her cats and chicken until she died in 1964. Today the area has an eerie, haunted feeling of desolation.

One of the families who had been made homeless by the storm was Eliza Ann Trout, a fisherman's widow, and her daughters, Patience, Ella, Clara and Edith. After the death of their father the two elder sisters worked as farm labourers and fishermen. The two sisters had built the hotel with their own hands having bought a piece of land after the storm. Originally this was called Prospect House, they had even made over 8,000 concrete blocks themselves, if they wanted a job done they did it, adding an extension for 66 guests, digging a trench from the nearest spring quarter of a mile away to supply water. Ella was known all over the world as the Modern Grace Darling for during the First World War she rescued a seaman from a torpedoed merchant ship in the Bay for which she received the OBE. During the Second World War the hotel became the Headquarters for the Allied Forces for D-Day landings. Ella was what would be described today as 'with it' and Trouts had one of the first television sets in the area. Sadly Patience died on 11th April 1949 and Ella three years later aged 55 while visiting her father's grave. She was a fearless women of great resources who fished like any man in all weathers, sometimes she would captain a male seine net crew, selected by the men themselves, sometimes helping to catch a ton of mullet a day.

When both the sisters died Edith tried to keep the hotel going but in 1959 she closed it although the tables were kept set for dinner. She lived as a recluse for 17 years without water or electricity. When she died in 1975 the hotel had virtually remained unchanged since 1959. It was made into holiday flats and a tea room. Now once again it is a hotel and re named Prospect so the wheel has gone full circle.

Of Hallsands virtually nothing is left now but ruins. Its story is told to students and school children as one of the finest British examples of what can happen as a result of tampering with little understood natural effects and ignorant bureaucracy.

Coastal erosion is one of the major challenges of the environment in the area. It ranges from the wearing away of the grass cover by the feet of admiring visitors along stretches of the coastal footpath, to the threat of destruction of whole villages such as Beesands and Torcross and ruins of Hallsands stand as witness to the power of the sea.

Recent sea-defence works at nearby Torcross and Beesands have been designed to prevent the same fate befalling these villages, perched similarly precariously on the very fringe of the sea. Many tons of boulders have been dropped at sea to try to restore the natural balance and sea-breaking capacity of the shingle bank which used to protect the coast.

Start Point.

Start Bay Inn

TORCROSS. KINGSBRIDGE.
Telephone: (01548) 580553

To describe the location of this lovely inn would be like trying to describe the gateway to Heaven! The long sweep of Slapton Sands finds Torcross to the south, before the road turns inland to Kingsbridge. Here at this ancient thatched inn, which stands on the ocean's tide, you will find a timeless hospitality. Real Ales along with real 'live' cider, which continues to ferment in the barrel, and crackling log fires make this an inn for all seasons! Paul and Fay Stubbs have been here for nearly 18 years, and have become known nationwide for the brilliance of the seafood dishes. Sea bass, haddock, skate, prawns, mussels and cockles, crabs and fresh caught plaice are offered together with a variety of other fine and original dishes. Vegetarian dishes too; a family room which welcomes children and everything is sensibly and reasonably priced. A good selection of wines complement the food, with new world wines and bin ends to widen your choice. Open every day from 11.30 am - 2.30 pm and 6.00 pm to 11.00 pm (winter) and open half an hour earlier in summer. No credit cards. Tips? If you like - but here's one from me - try the fish pie! This inn gets Woody's award of Excellence.

The SHIP AND PLOUGH

THE PROMENADE. KINGSBRIDGE. S. DEVON.
Telephone: (01548) 853485

Now here's an inn for the man (or woman - let's not be sexist) who really loves good beer! Supreme champion at the Cardiff Beer Festival with a staggeringly (if you will forgive the expression) good stout. The Ship and Plough houses Blewitts Brewery with ales ranging from 3.8 to 6.00 (1060 sg) aptly named Blewitts Trumpet, Blewitts Headoff, Blewitts Nose and Blewitts Wages. Gimmicks - NO WAY ... this is the real thing. The names are fun. The landlord, whose name is Blewitt, is a member of the Institute of Innkeepers, and he runs a fine lively inn.

Live entertainment on Friday and Sunday evenings, pub games; this is a family inn of character, a town centre inn and one with plenty of bustle and life. There is a good spacious functions room and a 40 seat restaurant featuring English and continental fare. If a locally produced beer can be this good, and this reasonable, many major brewers should be ashamed.

START POINT
TO KINGSBRIDGE

Since 1836 when its lamp was first lighted, Start lighthouse standing on Start Point has been a welcoming sight for returning sailors, its name coming from the Saxon word steort meaning tail. The actual lamp equivalent of 800,000 candlepower has a range of just over 20 miles. Sadly now automation no longer permits a tour of the lighthouse.

From here to the mouth of the Salcombe estuary leading up to Kingsbridge estuary and town, lies a stretch of breathtaking coastline with coves and beaches. However the lanes leading down to these are extremely narrow and twisty and not for nervous drivers. Lannacombe is the first village you reach and beyond is Prawle Point, the most southern point of Devon five miles further on. The cottages at Prawle were once the background for an extraordinary scene. In 1872 the Italian vessel, Marie Theresa out of Genoa, collided in the darkness with a strange ship which carried on without stopping. The Marie, badly holed headed on to shore whilst the Salcombe lifeboat went to her help. But the Master, Nicolo Bozzo would not let the pilot on board. Twelve of the crew reached Lannacombe in their own boat and were quartered at the Inn at East Prawle where, the worse for drink, it seems a quarrel broke out, one man produced a knife and stabbed several of his shipmates. In such a small village there was no policeman and the landlord turned to the coastguard for help as he was the only uniformed man in the area! He was also wounded and then the man with the knife ran to the coastguard cottages seeking further revenge, threatened another coastguard and his wife before an officer at the station killed him with a cutlass.

Lannacombe Bay.

What the quarrel was about, or what vessel it was that caused the sinking of the Italian boat was never discovered.

Literally hundreds of shipwrecks have occurred in this area including many warships. The 'Formidable' , a battleship of 15,000 tons sank with heavy losses on New Year's Day in 1915, hit by a torpedo from the German U boat U 24. The 'Formidable' sank in just 45 minutes and only three lifeboats could be launched. One capsized, a second with seventy men got clear and was later rescued by a light cruiser, and the third with sixty men made for Lyme Regis, Dorset. By the time Lyme was reached nine had died from their wounds and exposure. One was found barely alive suffering badly from hypothermia. His dog had saved his life by lying on the piece of sacking which covered him and kept him warm. Many German submarines were destroyed too. Some years after the war on 12th November 1925 our own M1 put out to sea and failed to surface somewhere off Start Point, never to be recovered. The Hotel at Gara Rock was once a coastguard station standing above a beautiful beach. Access in this area to the beaches is not too easy but the roads do run fairly close to the cliff paths and the longest walk is not more than quarter of a mile, the effort really being worth it for the clean sand, clear water and enchanting rock pools. East Portlemouth offers a sheltered beach a little way off the main holiday hubbub and beyond here Kingsbridge lies at the head of the estuary. All along the banks are creeks and inlets, each with a country pub - and a charm of its own. They can be explored by boat, on foot or by road. Two of these are South Pool after which a pack of Harriers was named, no one seems to know why - and Frogmore which means the lake or mere of frogs.

The Kingsbridge/Salcombe estuary is sometimes called a river, but actually it is a ria or drowned river valley which is tidal but not fed by any river. Small streams run under Kingsbridge into it making channels in the mud flats, exposed at low tide. At high tide boats and yachts sail up to Kingsbridge, made up of two mediaeval towns, Dodbrooke and Kingsbridge, and these moor at the quays as the tall ships did years ago.

Overlooking Lannacombe Bay.

KINGSBRIDGE

The town is said to have got its name from the fact that a Saxon king, on reaching Dodbrooke during his travels, could not cross the stream, so a volunteer from one of the local families walked across the Dod with the king on his back.

Fore Street, Kingsbridge.

Like Totnes, Kingsbridge offers the visitor ample car parking, the most convenient one being alongside the estuary, which apart from making an ideal place to observe the estuary's wildlife also offers access to the family sports centre. The town has a long history; mentioned in a charter of 962, and in 1219 the Abbot of Buckfast Abbey to whom the town belonged at the time, granted it a market. It became a borough in 1238 and a market centre for the surrounding countryside, to which the farmers still come. The main street, Fore street, runs steeply up from the estuary and before the car park was built at the bottom and the estuary filled in, the quays were busy with packet steamers. The paddle steamer which ran from Salcombe also berthed here whilst many fishing boats bobbed at anchor. The estuary's mediaeval trade was with the wine growing region of Southern France, the ships carried cargoes of every sort back and forth all over the world. During the 19th century shiploads of oranges, pineapples and coconuts were brought from the Azores, the Mediterranean and the West Indies - sugar and rum were carried in the swift little clippers which acquired a reputation for always being first home, although they were less well known than the tea clippers. These tall masted ships would often creep secretively into native waters in the hope of getting their cargoes to London before the news of their homecoming reached their rivals who might forestall them.

Schooners such as 'The Fanny' were built in Dodbrooke in 1850. William Date had learned the craft of shipbuilding at Salcombe and in 1847 started to build ships on his own account. In those days they didn't draw designs, they made moulds and the one of the Kingsbridge clipper still exists. The coming of the steel ships put an end to Kingsbridge as a prominent port and gradually it became a holiday area with small industrial units, as well of course, remaining a farming centre as it had always been.

The town has produced many famous sons including John Walcot later known as Peter Pindar, the satirical versifier who was born in Kingsbridge in the 18th century and went to the local Grammar School, as did W H Squire who became a founder scholar at the Royal School of Music when it opened in 1883. He wrote the 'pop' music of his time played by the world famous Celeste Octet. Two of his most famous songs were 'Loves Dream' and 'An Old Fashioned Town', in which he wrote of "an old fashioned house in an old fashioned town... I love every mouse in that old fashioned house in an old fashioned street that runs up and now down". This of course refers to Fore Street in Kingsbridge. Thomas Crispin was born here in 1608, making his fortune, as did so many, from cloth, but he never forgot the town of his birth and a plaque over the door of the old school commemorates its building in 1670 at his expense. The most famous of all is William Cookworthy and in a 17th century building near the top of Fore Street stands the Cookworthy Museum, sign-posted the Rural Life Museum, one of the most comprehensive and beautifully set out and equipped museums in the area. His mother was Cornish and his father a weaver, he was born at Dodbrooke in 1705, his father died when William was only thirteen and at fifteen he walked to London and was apprenticed to an apothecary but in 1726 returned to Devon and set up a partnership as a chemist under the sign Bevan and Cookworthy. He became interested in ceramics and experimented with the china clay found in the area, discovering petuntze and kaolin near Penzance. By 1768 he was satisfied with his experiments on the glazing of porcelain and took out a patent which led to a major industry in Devon and Cornwall.

One room in the museum is devoted to his work with many beautiful examples of early porcelain. There is also a complete Victorian kitchen, an Edwardian pharmacy, a farm gallery and a walled garden. Each year a local village is featured. A notice in the farm gallery reads: "The South Hams measured its own corn in sacks, and its land in farthings unlike anywhere else in Devon. It had its own breed of cattle and its own breed of sheep, and also its own variety of apple, the White Sour, famous for its cider."

On show too are the world famous Lidstone Stoves and ranges, a maritime section, and a collection of clothes from the past, Lidstone Stoves are even found in Newfoundland today.

Part way up Fore Street stands the town hall with its three sided clock, built in 1875. It has one blank side turned to face the inmates of the Union or Workhouse, although it is not clear why it was thought the inmates should be unaware of the time. A little further on stand the Shambles Butterwalk built in

1585, once housing butcher's stalls and a corn market. These were saved from demolition when The Cheape was removed to allow carts and carriages to pass when they took the place of packhorses. The Cheape was a large wooden market building in the middle of the street with the pillory beside it, and on market days there were stalls, and animals for sale.

St. Edmunds Church stands behind the Shambles dating from the 13th to 15th centuries. Outside stands the well known slab bearing the epitaph of Robert Phillips:

> *"Here I lie at the Chancel Door,*
> *Here lie I because I am poor,*
> *The further in the more you pay*
> *Here lie I as warm as they."*

Opposite stands the Kings Arms built in 1775 and from here coaches and carriers' wagons set out. Although we think our roads are dangerous today, in the 19th century there were just as serious coach accidents and it is no wonder when you read of the tricks the drivers got up to trying to race each other and cut seconds off their time - tipping over, slashing with their whips, passing and repassing with much blowing of horns - the 'yard of tin'. Here one enterprising landlord grew his own lemons for the warming punch the passengers needed. In 1824 when Robert Foale owned the Inn he ran a twice weekly service of post chaise to Plymouth known as the Telegraph. Here in 1870 stood the first billiard table in Kingsbridge and further up the street where once the Albion Hotel stood the first motor car ever seen in Kingsbridge drew up outside on 7th October, 1898.

There are too many Inns in the town to mention each by name, but they all provide first class home cooked food from local produce and offer a warm welcome to visitors.

On Monday 18th December, 1893 the railway came to Kingsbridge from South Brent. Everyone had a half day holiday, bunting hung in the streets, there were torchlight processions with all the trimmings, but sadly it was too late, for the motor car was on its way and after only seventy years the last train entered the station with a garland round its funnel, the old station now being an industrial estate.

Apart from the local cider, part of Devon's heritage, White Ale was once famous here and in 1897 it was written about thus: "..there is another liquor on which the thirsty traveller can fall back, somewhat uninviting in appearance it is true, but of very high and ancient repute in Kingsbridge where it is chiefly made. If it be true indeed as many have held - White Ale was once the staple diet of Western England - what is this delectable drink? That is declared to be a secret known only to one family and jealously guarded through successive generations, all the outer world knows is that eggs are in it as well as some mystical ingredient called 'grout'; it flies quickly to the head...it looks like some extremely nauseous doctor's draught...it would be a rare and monumental folly to lose cider and retain White Ale." Evidently the writer's advice was followed.

Many people think of Kingsbridge as the capital of the South Hams and certainly all roads lead to it and there is much to do and see. The shops are first class offering everything from four poster beds to smoked fish and home made pasties, fashionable clothes and everything for the sportsman and woman. It is an ideal centre from which to enjoy all the surrounding unspoilt villages and countryside. Golf courses in the area abound, there is horse riding, trout fishing and it is a natural haven for walkers and those who want to go down to the sea or river in any kind of vessel. At the Sports Centre there is something for everyone from aerobics, squash, volley ball, bowls and 50+ activities. Situated by the Quay is the Tourist Information Centre. There are facilities nearby for canoe courses under qualified instruction in safe local creeks. The Recreation Ground, once a tidal millpond offers tennis, putting and bowls and even in November there is Magic Saturday, the day of the Kingsbridge Extravaganza when all traffic is banned from the town and the streets become one gigantic party with a funfair on the Quay; Christmas illuminations are switched on, and the day ends with community singing with the Silver Band on the Quay. As you walk round the town the modern facades of some of the shops tend to hide the true antiquity of the buildings, often revealed when you go inside. There are many side passages leading off Fore Street, most of which reveal something of great interest - an old archway of an abbot's house - little courtyards and cottages bright with flowers, a Baptist Church. At the bottom of Fore Street behind the Ship and Plough is found the Anchor shopping centre and Malthouse Craft Centre. During the summer a launch sails regularly between Kingsbridge and Salcombe and in July the Fair comes to town when many cattle and sheep are sold in the market. This traditional Fair has been held since 1461. There are two weekly markets on the Quay. All in all there is literally something here to appeal to everyone whatever age or choice.

There are many 18th century houses, some slate hung, in the local style, an obvious result of the hundreds of small slate quarries in the area, one of the best known is at Charleton south of Kingsbridge on the Torcross road. This slate was used all over Devon for farm boundary walls and roofing slates, which became more beautiful with the weathering of years, producing moss and lichens. During the 18th century much of this was exported to Holland.

The slate from Charleton used to be loaded at Tacket Wood Quay sometimes known as Ticket Wood from the days of religious persecution when non-conformists were admitted to their illicit meeting places by ticket only.

Before we leave Kingsbridge mention must be made of an event which put the town on the sports pages of all the Sunday newspapers back in April 1991. The locally trained racehorse Seagram won the Grand National at Aintree. Ridden by Nigel Hawke, and trained by the now retired David Barons just outside Kingsbridge, Seagram won at odds of 12/1 having also won the Ritz Club Chase at the Cheltenham Festival meeting three weeks earlier. Upon his return to the South Hams he was given a tremendous welcome and all roads to Kingsbridge were congested with well-wishers eager to greet their local hero.

As is so often the case with Grand National winners, an interesting little story surrounded Seagram and his connections. The 1991 National was sponsored by 'Seagram' the whisky distillers, and their chairman Ivan Straker was offered ownership of 'Seagram the thoroughbred' several years previously. The offer was turned down and when the horse won the Grand National he was jointly owned by David Barons his trainer and Sir Eric Parker. The winning owners were presented their trophy by Ivan Straker. If he had accepted the offer of ownership the possibility of presenting and receiving the trophy by and to the same person would have arisen, and Seagram would have won the 'Seagram Grand National' for 'Seagram the sponsors'.

STOKELEY FARM SHOP

STOKELEY BARTON. STOKENHAM. KINGSBRIDGE.
Tel: (01548) 580372(Farm) or (01548) 581010 (Shop)

This superb farm shop offers a full range of fruit and vegetables including fresh, homegrown and locally grown produce whenever possible. There is a range of wholefoods, conserves, dairy produce and a gift shop. The plant centre offers homegrown bedding plants and a speciality is the interesting range of patio plants and hanging baskets. Roses, perennials, shrubs, conifers and cut flowers are also on sale. Fine views of Start Bay can be seen from the pick-your-own facility which has the usual range of soft fruits, apples, plums and a selection of vegetables throughout the season. Coffee shop, plenty of parking and access for wheelchairs

HAZELWOOD HOUSE

LODDISWELL. NR. KINGSBRIDGE. DEVON.
Telephone: (01548) 821232

This fine original country house is both a country hotel and a retreat. It is set in 67 acres of river valley, and is dedicated to being a place of peace and tranquillity. There are special musical events during the year, and a rich programme of creative course, concerts and special events of many kinds. There are 16 rooms in Hazelwood itself, plus four letting cottages - self catering if you wish - on short term (a week to a month). Excellent food ... mostly organic, but not vegetarian...although vegetarians are well catered for. No credit cards. Must be seen to be really appreciated; Hazelwood is something very special. Send for Brochure.

Buckland-Tout-Saints

KINGSBRIDGE. DEVON.

Telephone: (01548) 853055 Fax: (01548) 856261

USA International Freephone: 1.800.435.8281

Buckland-Tout-Saints is simply exquisite. An elegant Queen Anne manor house, set in the depth of rural Devon, it stands in six acres of landscaped gardens. This twelve roomed gem of a country hotel offers an almost forgotten standard of personal service which is created by the owners John and Tove Taylor and their son George. Renowned for excellent food, the menus feature the very best of locally grown fresh produce together with the best game, poultry, meat and fish prepared by the team of skilled chefs. Fillet of sea bream, roast lamb and braised saddle of rabbit, join venison and pheasant on ever-changing dishes which take full advantage of the season's best choice, and both the starters and desserts are equally tempting. A true Devon country retreat. The Hotel has won two AA rosettes for cuisine and service, and three merit awards from the RAC. Brochure available.

The UNION INN

Chillington. Nr. Kingsbridge. S. Devon. Tel: (01548) 580241

It is always a pleasure to discover an inn that has not been "tastefully modernised" (usually meaning wall-to-wall plastic seating). Such is the Union Inn in the village of Chillington. In times past, illegal union meetings were held here. The inn is totally unspoiled. Big log fires crackle in the hearth, and the wafts of home-cooking delight the taste-buds. Wonderful steak & kidney pie is often on the menu, and the best of local poultry and fish are featured on the blackboard specials. In the summer you can enjoy salads outside in the garden, where the views are simply lovely. The inn has Real Ales and a vegetarian selection as well as the usual menu and bar snacks. Just 5 minutes from Slapton Sands or Blackpool Sands.

The **CRABSHELL INN**

EMBANKMENT ROAD. KINGSBRIDGE. DEVON.
Telephone: (01548) 852345

This delightful inn stands at the water's edge and has its own private moorings on the river so that you may arrive by boat. There are riverside tables, and the slap of the water and clink of the sheets against the masts of moored boats adds so much to the wonderful atmosphere of the Crabshell. Wheelchair access, extensive vegetarian meals and children very welcome (a fully equipped games room will amuse them) make this a family inn par excellence. Fresh seafood is a speciality, but the varied menu features steaks, grills and dishes like lasagne. The special lobster platter and crab platter (for two people) are great favourites, as is the seafood platter. The lobster is served with mackerel, king prawns, a seafood cocktail, crab claws and prawns as an example of the generosity of these platters, and they taste as delightful as they look! There is a separate children's menu and prices are sensible and realistic. The main menu includes cold platters, jacket potato selections, salads, home-made specialities, grills and even some Indian cuisine dishes. There is a large car park and the inn accepts Visa and Mastercard. Real Ales - Real Atmosphere!

THE SLOOP INN

BANTHAM. NR. KINGSBRIDGE. S. DEVON.
Tel: (01548) 560215 Tel/Fax: (01548) 560489

Over a century ago this ancient smuggler's inn was featured in a London newspaper. Before the advent of the motor car, they spoke of the time it took to arrive at the Sloop "trotting through the country lanes"! One used to arrive by horse and carriage then, and in truth, the welcome would have been no warmer than todays. The inn is one of the loveliest I have ever found. Superb in summer…and just as good in winter, here you will find the very best home-cooked fare, featuring fish, shellfish, crabs and steaks from an a la carte menu complemented by daily specials on the blackboard. Scallops Mornay and salmon with a white wine and prawn sauce vie for your attention, together with trout, brill, dover sole or halibut - on a bed of leeks and bacon.

The inn once belonged to a famous South Hams smuggler and wrecker, and landlord Neil Girling has many stories of those days. There are 5 en suite double bedrooms - including 2 family rooms, and three separate cottages which are available to rent. Telephone for the brochure.

One of the finest beaches in the whole of the west country is but a few minutes stroll down the lane, and the whole area is remote, peaceful and totally unspoiled, with some fine coastal paths. Bantham is located just $2\frac{1}{2}$ miles off the A279 by Churchstow. A magical place, filled with tranquillity and a feeling of times past.

QUALITY PRODUCE
SOUTH HAMS

MEMBER OF THE
SOUTH HAMS FOOD &
DRINK ASSOCIATION

SALCOMBE
TO BOLBERRY DOWN

If visiting Salcombe during the holiday months then we strongly recommend using the park and ride facility on the outskirts of the town. The streets are narrow and easily congested and the main car park, which doubles as a boat park in winter, soon fills up.

After the Second World War Salcombe became a lotus eating area for men returning from the hell of war they had known, with gratuities to spend and borrowed time which they had not expected. Some took up shell-fishing, apparently an idyllic easy way of life, most of them were soon disillusioned when they discovered hauling lobster and crab pots was no easy option involving long hours and bad weather. Others bought luxury yachts for charter, cafes, pubs and restaurants as life appeared to be one perpetual summer, and Salcombe lent itself favourably to idleness and enjoyment, the climate is one of the mildest in England and some people have even grown oranges and lemons out of doors; in fact it has often been compared with towns beside the Mediterranean. The estuary is crowded with boats of every description from canoes to luxury yachts, and as mentioned the roads with cars, but it is certainly one of the most ideal places in which to learn to sail as the estuary which runs up to Kingsbridge is safe and either side is some of the most beautiful countryside in Devon where meadows and trees sweep down to the water and there are small sandy coves and secret creeks crowded with bird life. The Island Cruising Club is one of the UK's largest sailing schools and has been providing a wide range of sailing holidays and courses since 1952. There are marinas to service boats - many of which can be hired, as well as privately owned, the water is as crowded with vessels as a motorway with vehicles! From here such people as Chay Blyth and Rod and Naomi James set off on their record breaking trips.

The car park doubles as a boat park in winter.

Approaching by road down Church Hill, at sea level you reach Fore Street, the narrow thoroughfare leading through the town to Bolt Head and the open sea. The water is blue, the walls of the buildings are white, half close your eyes and you are in Algiers. The town held the honour of being the last place in Devon to hold out for the King in the Civil War and at North Sands is Salcombe Castle or Fort Charles, a battered shell of its old self on a rock surrounded by sea, built in the reign of Henry VIII against French and Spanish marauders. It witnessed a four month seige through the spring of 1646, actually only one person on either side was killed and at the end of the war sixty six men and two laundresses marched out beating drums with their colours flying.

In the middle of the 19th century the travellers to Devon had begun to notice something new, a change - the start of what was to become the county's most important money spinner - the holiday industry. In those days Exeter people mostly holidayed in Exmouth or Teignmouth, beyond Dartmouth only tiny fishing villages existed - Salcombe was the only place known, its name arising from the word saltern which was a shed in which during the 11th century salt was made from evaporating brine.

In the 1500s Salcombe supplied ships to join the Fleet, and in 1588 towns and villages round about fitted out sixteen ships to join the defence against the Armada. From time immemorial the perfect natural harbour was used for the start of sea-going activity. For centuries sloops, brigs and schooners were built in the yards by people like the Cook family who were both boat builders and fishermen.

They themselves went crabbing in a 34ft boat with two hundred pots, setting them three miles off Prawle Point, some of the bigger boats would take 500 pots a trip. As the fishing industry grew so did piracy and smuggling, men hiding in the wooded inlets and coves to sail out and plunder passing ships, and it was not unknown for local fishermen to take a hand in this.

Views across the estuary from Salcombe.

After the defeat of the Armada it was mostly fishing craft which were built in the town, then the trade increased rapidly over the years and 1864 marked the height of the Salcombe/Kingsbridge shipbuilding and trading prosperity.

In that year there were as many as ninety eight foreign-going ships and an equal number of coasting and harbour vessels. Shipyards grew up along the present harbour front accompanied by sailmakers, chandlers and carpenters. Fruit clippers were the speciality and farmers and manufacturers in the district sent their food and goods to market in fast topsail schooners, which also carried general cargoes from port to port. They brought back cargoes of cocoa, timber, wine, rubber and silk from foreign ports. Many of the fruit clippers bore the names of their native villages and rivers - Salcombe Castle, Avon, Malborough, West Alvington. The air of the little town must have smelled of pitch, tar and wood shavings and been loud with the sound of axe, saw and hammer, all of which were needed to keep the ships in tip top condition. You can imagine the streets full of swaggering seamen with their salt and sunburned faces, their long hair surmounted by woollen tasselled caps - perhaps there isn't much change now except the men own the boats and don't just sail in them!

As to the pirates, it was a paradise for them as the town was almost inaccessible from the land, and dominated the shipping lanes in the channel, and no one thought any the worse of the men who mixed both legitimate and illegitimate trading; in fact legend has it that the Rector of Portlemouth, where the church looks across the estuary, one Sunday faltered in his sermon, and them stopped altogether, tearing off his surplice he shouted to the congregation, "My brethren there is a wreck on the Bar! But let us all start fair." The sea captains of Salcombe grew wealthy and built themselves solid Victorian villas along the elegant curve of Devon Road, and by the end of the 19th century there were two hundred three masted ships in the harbour. But with the coming of other methods of ship building, the trade dwindled and by the beginning of the First World War there was little shipbuilding apart from dinghies and fishing boats by such people as the Cove family who built whalers for the Navy. Only five trading vessels were registered in Salcombe and these

were all owned outside the district. Although fishing and boatbuilding are no longer great industries, the neighbouring channel waters are some of the richest shellfish grounds off Britain and the modern crab industry reached enormous proportions, all types of shellfish being taken to London and other parts of Britain.

One of the most interesting features of Salcombe is the lifeboat with its list of rescues and assistance of every kind. Their area stretches from Torbay to the Yealm and 30 miles out to sea. The RNLI established a station here in 1869, the year the Cutty Sark was launched, and the station has a long and interesting record of rescues of every kind. 1932 was one of the busiest with six launches. On 15th October 1935, Flying Boat S1299 from RAF Calshot made a forced descent off Start and the lifeboat towed the boat and crew into Dartmouth. In 1870 a lifeboat house was built and in 1916 came the greatest tragedy of all. On 27th October the William and Emma was launched in a furious gale to go to the assistance of a Plymouth schooner, the Western Lass which had gone ashore in Lannacombe Bay. In spite of almost insurmountable difficulties Coxswain Edwin Distin got the boat out over the sand bar at the mouth of the estuary although everyone had said it was madness to launch. In the meantime a message had come to Salcombe to say the Prawle rocket company had saved the schooner's crew, but in those days there was no way of letting the lifeboat know of this and she went on into the dark, stormy autumn dawn. When they reached the wreck they realised what had happened and turned to make for harbour. As they approached Salcombe a huge wave caught them and threw the boat high into the air, followed by another which capsized her. In spite of the men on shore making every effort to get a breeches buoy to them, only two men survived, Edwin Distin and William Johnson. To a small community the loss of 13 lives was a terrible blow.

Between 1930 and 1938 the boat named the Alfred and Clara Heath was put on reserve when Salcombe got their new one, the Marie Parkhouse. The Alfred and Clara was sent to Guernsey to operate. Meanwhile the Germans occupied the island and the boat was captured by them, the only known case of a British RNLI boat being taken by the enemy! The waiting area for the ferry across to East Portlemouth displays the Salcombe Lifeboat's rescue and service record.

The permanent population of Salcombe is not as large as might be expected, in 1992 it was approximately 3,000, but it can double or treble in the summer and nowadays sailing and going down to the sea in ships in every type of boat is the stock in trade of the town and has come to dominate the scene. The shops are mostly to be found along the waterfront and they cater for every taste, many of the hotels and guest houses nestle in wooded precincts and the two principal sandy beaches are North Sands and South Sands, both long famous for swimming and sunbathing. They have the attraction of being sheltered by the Bar across the harbour entrance, and North Sands has toilet and refreshment facilities, with the added convenience of having the town close at hand.

On the eastern side of the estuary a series of sandy coves can be reached by the East Portlemouth pedestrian ferry. The Town Regatta was established in 1857 and becomes more and more popular each year with events ranging from vintage gig racing to a torchlight procession, taking place during the first week in August. There is a warm welcome for yachtsmen and women at Salcombe Yacht Club. There is a Dive Centre so you can see the other half of Salcombe under water! Dozens of firms hire out boats from canoes to yachts and will give tuition. You can water ski, there is a Watersports Centre with everything to do with water activity on offer, you can charter a yacht with or without crew, and there are chandlers and sports shops and other pastimes.

The Salcombe Maritime and Local History Museum is in the basement of the town hall in Market Street. Here are photographs, paintings, maps, models and ship building tools showing Salcombe's history as a sailing ship port in the 19th century and as an American base during the Second World War, as well as a diving exhibition.

The town has much to offer, its beaches, coastal walks, water sports, and many unusual shops tucked away up tiny side streets along with a wide choice of pubs and restaurants. Fish on the menu features strongly in the restaurants with dressed crab, lobster, oysters, prawns, escallops and also some of the very best locally made ice cream to be found.

For anyone interested in painting and pictures there are numerous exhibitions at the Salcombe Art Club in the Loft Studios near the waterfront with resident artists, here you can browse among the pictures and perhaps choose one as a holiday souvenir.

Near the boat hard and harbour office in the middle of Salcombe is a bronze plaque commemorating the 50th anniversary of D-Day. 6/6/44. Sixty six ships of the US Navy and many other auxiliary ships sailed out into the English channel to take part in the allied landings on the Normandy beaches. Perhaps as a visitor you may look across the shining water and think for a moment of all those shadowy figures of both the near and distant past who kept this harbour safe for present enjoyment, many of whom never returned to its shelter.

Along the cliffs from Bolt Head to Bolt Tail above Hope Cove, hundreds of wrecks have been charted, but it is also an area of some of the most beautiful and inaccessible south coast of Devon and the area has been listed as one of outstanding natural beauty, which is believable if you stand on Bolt Head and look at the view spread around. At your feet is Starehole Bay, a reminder of one of the most dramatic of all wrecks when the last of the large square riggers, a Finnish four masted barque the Herzogin Cecilie carrying a cargo of Australian wheat was wrecked on 25th April 1936. This was her last passage in the unofficial grain race from Australia. Known as The Duchess as her figurehead was the Duchess Cecilie, daughter of the Duke of Oldenberg, she was on her way to Ipswich to discharge her cargo. Early in the morning in thick fog and rough sea she touched the Ham Stone near Soar Mill Cove. Pamela Eriksson, wife of the captain, had had a premonition of disaster in a dream from which she woke crying "She's on the rocks!" and it proved to be right. The ship was holed in the forepeak at 4 am, 10 miles off her intended track the next day. How she came to be there no one will ever know. Later, Captain Sven Eriksson wrote to the Receiver of Wrecks "Loss due to fog and possible magnetic attraction from the cliffs." This is not as far fetched as it may sound as it may have thrown the compass and this has been reported along here many times before. The Salcombe lifeboat stood by for three hours and eventually took off one lady passenger and 21 of the 30 crew. Eventually the wreck was beached in Starehole Bay, the grain still in her hold, which gradually seeped out to the bird's delight but not those of the residents in Salcombe who had to live with the stinking, rotting grain on their beaches for a year or more. In the September she was sold for scrap for £225; her figurehead and barometer donated to the maritime museum in Alnds in Finland. In January 1939 she broke up into four pieces and the cabin and other remains can be seen in The Cottage Hotel in Hope Cove. Pamela Eriksson wrote a book 'The Duchess', telling the whole story of the ship's life and death.

The people who came best out of the disaster were the farmers who owned the land on the cliffs above the wreck where literally thousands of people came to look at the boat and paid to park their cars, so perhaps one can say it is an ill wind …

Before leaving Salcombe one more place not to be missed is Overbecks Museum and Gardens. To reach it you walk up the hill past Splat Cove below

Bolt Head Hotel which brings you to the start of the Round Walk, the road ending at the National Trust car park next to the Museum and Gardens.

Dr. Otto Overbeck was a research chemist, who died in 1937 and left the house, its grounds and his collections to the National Trust. There are six acres of gardens, peaceful and heady with perfume from the shrubs and flowers. The garden has banana palms, syringa, olives, camphor, fuschia and azaleas, a prize magnolia is the centre of attraction when it flowers. Inside the museum are model ships and shipwrights' tools, local photographs, shells, butterflies and birds. A secret door for children hides a magical collection of childhood objects, dolls and toys, and there is a 103 years old polyphon. The museum won the Gulbenkian Prize - best provision for children. There is also a shop and tea room.

From Bolt Head the next village you come to inland is Bolberry, once said to be a sporting venue for some kind of horse racing known as the Kingsbridge Annual Diversions. This seems to have been a somewhat movable occasion ending up in Totnes as a steeplechase. There is also a delightful Donkey Sanctuary in a beautiful garden setting with donkey rides, goats, peacocks and other exotic birds. Years ago there was a nine hole golf course with a very up market clubhouse. This was to be extended to 18 holes but never took off. It's history can be seen on the walls of the Port Light restaurant which took over the clubhouse.

SALCOMBE DAIRY

SHADYCOMBE ROAD. SALCOMBE. DEVON. **Tel: (01548) 843228**

"Wherever they care about the quality of food and drink - you are likely to find Salcombe Dairy Ice Cream."

A simple statement, but it perfectly represents the policies of this major dairy ice-cream producer. The flavours are entirely natural: e.g. Cherry Brandy contains De Kuypers and black cherries; the blackcurrant has over a pound of blackcurrants in every gallon.

This superb ice cream is available from local retail shops and delicatessens and in restaurants, hotels and National Trust properties throughout the west country. Ask for it by name. Salcombe Real Dairy Ice Cream.

Woody's verdict: MOUTHWATERING

HERON HOUSE HOTEL

THURLESTONE SANDS. NR. SALCOMBE. DEVON.
Telephone: (01548) 561308

Here is sheer magic! Set in one of the most enchanting locations you could ever imagine, this truly gorgeous small hotel commands a seascape that has to be seen to be believed. Standing just above the water's edge, it overlooks the Thurlestone Rock and a sandy beach, a National Trust property, that has earned a gold plaque for safety and cleanliness. The 60 seater restaurant is renowned for good food - and is open to non-residents every evening from 7.15pm. (Last orders 8.30pm and do book in advance!) There are eighteen bedrooms - all en suite with colour T.V., phone, radio and tea/coffee making facilities, and all have lovely views of the sea and/or countryside. There is a spacious swimming pool, heated from May through to September, and waiter service is available throughout the day, as you relax, swim and just bask! Situated close to Salcombe, Hope Cove, and Kingsbridge, there are golf courses, beaches, water sport facilities, walking, fishing and horse riding all within easy reach. This is an hotel with a real feeling of HOLIDAY .... and a friendly relaxed atmosphere where children and dogs are also welcome .

The Heron House Hotel has won the South Hams for all Seasons Award and the Premier Good Beach Award and Woody's Award of Excellence for fine food and wine. There can hardly be an hotel in a lovelier location if you enjoy a natural setting. There is a wildlife sanctuary directly opposite the hotel, and the views are incomparable. The hotel is family owned and run, and in every aspect - it shows! What finer recommendation?

The South Sands Hotel

SALCOMBE. TQ8 8LL.   TELEPHONE: (01548) 843741

This jewel of the South Hams is the sister hotel to the long established family owned Tides Reach Hotel, which is also featured in this guide. The South Sands however, is very much a FAMILY hotel, located right on the beach and offering 30 rooms and family suites, all with colour television, radio, direct dial phones, hairdryers, tea/coffee making facilities and a baby listening service. There is a heated swimming pool, restaurant and a pub type Terrace bar serving food and Real Ales - (open to non-residents).

Safe bathing, boating and water-sports; fishing, surfing and sailing are all an integral part of what The South Sands has to offer. The beaches are among the safest and cleanest in Britain, and the friendly/helpful staff are chosen for their caring attitude to the family. The Edwards family take great pride in the ambience and friendliness of both hotels, and particularly at The South Sands, to the facilities which make children so very welcome. The South Sands also has a shallow indoor pool, children's playroom, solarium and steam room. (A squash court, multi gym and snooker table are available in the adjacent Tides Reach).

Tides Reach Hotel

SOUTH SANDS. SALCOMBE. TQ8 8LJ   **Tel: (01548) 843466**

Owned by the Edwards family for some 30 years, the Tides Reach Hotel is one of the most attractive hotels I have ever had the pleasure to write about. Situated in a secluded wooded bay, the Tides Reach really does stand right at the edge of the sea. Thirty-eight bedrooms, all en suite, with facilities such as hair dryers, direct dial phones, colour televisions etc. feature exquisite colour co-ordinated furnishings, and the majority have panoramic sea views. A 90 seat restaurant is open throughout the year, and meals are also served in the garden and round the swimming pool.

The Aquarium bar is simply amazing, and the fish - some over four feet long, enjoy watching you watching them! Superb indoor swimming pool and leisure complex as well as a snooker room, sauna, solarium, hair/beauty salon and 'Whirlpool' spa bath. Golf, Tennis, riding, surfing, fishing and every other sport can be enjoyed within a few miles of South Sands, and the beach offers wind-surfing, water-skiing, sailing and canoeing. The hotel is renowned for its excellent food and first class selection of wines, and locally caught fish is always featured on the menus. The hotel has earned accolades from all the recognised guides, and the English Tourist Board has awarded the Tides Reach five crowns in their 'Highly Commended' category.

QUALITY PRODUCE
SOUTH HAMS
MEMBER OF THE
SOUTH HAMS FOOD &
DRINK ASSOCIATION

MODBURY
AND SURROUNDINGS

This is a beautiful mediaeval market town, still virtually unspoilt. Somehow it has come to terms tentatively between the modern age and its historic past, caught in a delightful time warp where you can still feel the atmosphere of the essence of the South Hams as it was, and still enjoy the amenities of today. This is most likely because in 1969 it was designated a Conservation Area so its character can be maintained for all to enjoy. Adequate car parking and an information centre are sign-posted in the town centre.

Modbury developed from a Saxon settlement and is full of history, much of which can be gleaned from a booklet 'A History of Modbury' published by the Local History Society; and from another equally delightful, 'The Life of a Country Thatcher,' a memoir by John Rogers, also presented by the same Society, so at least some of the past is preserved in print.

A steep hill runs up the centre of the town and many of the houses are 18th and 19th century, once the homes of prosperous wool merchants. The Champernowne family also had a mansion here and were lords of the manor and borough from the time of Edward II. It was a borough before 1238 with a weekly market and annual fair. Until the 1890s St George's Fair lasted nine days, and the ten inns kept open all day. It had been granted a market in 1155, the opening being marked by hoisting a white glove garlanded with flowers to symbolise free trading and leniency by the law, while alcohol was on sale from street traders and private householders. The glove is still shown at the opening of the May Fair held the first week in May.

The glove ceremony is in memory of a glove given by King John during a visit. Another custom was to hang a holly bush outside private houses to indicate they served as public houses. Cattle and other stock were sold in Broad Street, the only flat area of the town, the last sale being in 1944.

The 16th century timbered Exeter Inn is the pride of Broad Street, a striking building in black and white, once owned by a first class chef, Leslie Hoare, who, long before Keith Floyd had even thought of fish, used to prepare delicious dishes from Devon for television viewers, mouth watering banquets all from local produce which you could sample at his inn.

The merchants' houses in the town were created with a great deal of imagination and style. Old Traine House, an Elizabethan mansion was replaced by New Traine House with a 19th century pillared facade. This can be found a few hundred yards up Brownston Street on the left hand side. Brick House, located on the opposite side and a hundred yards or so nearer the town centre, was once a hat factory.

Modbury was twice fought over in the Civil War when a group of locals took a mercenary view of the situation and fought on the side which paid its supporters the most - a kind of collective Vicar of Bray situation. Parliamentary troops were billeted in the church of St George and defaced many of the effigies by hacking off their feet leaving one a mere torso.

This was the age of the Perpendicular style in England, Eton College became the benefactor of Modbury church with a fine peal of bells in which the town has always taken pride, even inspiring a piece of poetry:-

Hark the Modbury bells
How they do quiver
Better than Ermington
down by the river.

Katherine Champernowne who was the daughter of Sir Philip, married Otho Gilbert in 1531 from Compton Castle near Torquay. They had two sons, Sir Humphrey Gilbert, the founder of the colony of Newfoundland, and Adrian who discovered the North West Passage in 1584. Most famous of all was Sir Walter Raleigh, her son by her second husband, Walter Raleigh of Fardel, Devon. She is buried in the churchyard. At the north west end of the town is a stone enclosure where a barracks once stood for troops under canvas who had been mobilised for the Napoleonic wars.

Standing on top of the hill you can see three ridges running east to west where South Hams farmers used to drive their cattle up to the moor to save their precious grass in the lower fields for hay. This was possibly the route the Bronze Age Beaker people took after sailing over from the continent to make their way to Dartmoor to found their settlements.

Like most other towns and large villages, Modbury was self supporting for generations with nearly every trade and profession represented - the brothers Ashley had a tannery, Choakes a butchery business and between them these two provided employment for many of the local men. Thomas Fice made water wheels and three mills worked continuously; there was a blacksmith, wheelwright, shoemaker and saddler.

Thomas Savery, who was a friend of Isaac Newton, was born here in 1650. He was a clockmaker and engineer, his most important invention being a pump designed to pump water from the mines. During his life time he carried out many further inventions and just before his death in 1714 he was made Surveyor of the Water Works at Hampton Court. In the Victoria and Albert Museum stands the Mayne Swete clock made in 1705 for his brother Adrian of Traine in Modbury by Mayne Swete and is an outstanding example of the combination of clock and cabinet making in the early 19th century. It played tunes by means of a keyboard every three hours and on Sundays, a psalm.

The highest population recorded was in 1821 when it was over 2000, most of the inhabitants being employed in the wool trade; then the Industrial Revolution took the industry to Yorkshire so that fullers, tuckers, weavers, dyers and all the other people connected with wool, lost their jobs and an added blow occurred when the railway bypassed the town on its passage westwards.

Population figures tell a large part of the story of 19th century Modbury - in 1961 it was just 1077. The decline is due not only to the reasons given above, but also the decline in numbers of those engaged in agriculture, some of the work done by hand being mechanised, an increase in pasture land and people moving away for employment. Had the railway come it might have produced more industry.

A Charity school was founded in 1730 for poor boys, and a school built at Brownston in 1874; in 1827 The White Hart Hotel and assembly rooms at the bottom of Church Street were built, and in 1865 the Gasworks in the valley to the south of the town were constructed. They ceased working in 1930, and now sadly the White Hart stands empty.

Of course the car brought easier travel to the town for such places as Plymouth, Kingsbridge and Torbay, it also brought people into Modbury from the smaller villages in the neighbourhood, particularly as regards schooling. Much building has taken place, some by Kingsbridge Rural District Council and some by private enterprise. The Memorial Hall in Back Street was built in 1954 to commemorate the dead of two world wars and many of the beautiful old buildings are listed in the Ministry's List of Scheduled Buildings.

So what of Modbury today? There is much here to attract the visitor - for instance Modbury Court which is a shopping area with such places as Megabyte who supply pizzas made to suit all tastes and appetites. There is a kitchen shop, a jewellers, gift shop, delicatessen, flower shop, and a rather unusual wedding shop specialising in silk and includes everything for the bride and all her attendants, even the shoes can be made to match. In the Old Chapel in Church Street is a fascinating furniture shop with a difference, where a woodturner makes reproduction country furniture from cradles to step ladders for librarians to reach the top shelves! There is also an abundance of antique shops. At the top of the town is a small industrial estate. The tourist information office gives detail of nearby cottages to rent, sited on a small, historic sheep farm in the Erme valley near a sandy beach - which brings us to the places nearby which are very much worth a visit. Sea routes to Modbury were once much in use; all the ridged roads drop down towards the Erme to connect with landing places such as Wonwell, Orcheton Mill and Goutsford. These were used for the export of wool from the surrounding countryside and tin from Dartmoor, then later for imports of coal and limestone which was burnt in kilns in the area and spread on the fields. The slipway at Wonwell still exists and was in regular use until 1917, the other two are derelict.

Three and a half miles south of Modbury is the village of Kingston. The 14th century, slate built church has the lovely name of St James the Less. Nearby is the Dolphin Inn which functions both sides of the road, the old stables opposite the house itself have been made into holiday accommodation. This was originally used for stabling packhorses and donkeys with a loft above for storing hay. Recently the landlord linked the pub with the London Stock

Exchange so customers could check the state of the stock market. Apart from the fish from the river brought up in mauns, the baskets slung on the animals' backs, smuggling was one of the chief operations in this area when men would row across to France and return with barrels of spirits to Westcombe beach where they stored the contraband in caves from where a passage led to Scobbiscombe Farm which had a big moveable flagstone in the kitchen floor.

There are only approximately 300 inhabitants in the village today but even so they have their own fire brigade which was started by volunteers in the 1950s with a hand cart and stirrup pump. Much of the land once belonged to Lord Mildmay of Flete, the grounds of Flete being open to the public in the summer. One local resident whose family have lived in the village for over 200 years, remembers the pheasant shoots when her grandfather went 'brushing', turning up the birds in the days when they didn't use dogs. A lot of poaching went on by moonlight when men went out with nets and ferrets, they put the hares and rabbits in a basket covered with a cloth and sold them to local tradsmen. Many years ago the church was the centre of village life and Mrs Pittman used to play the organ, walking from where she lived in Modbury and so as not to waste time, she knitted stockings as she walked.

There were no holidays then, but day outings to Bournemouth, Weston Super Mare and St Ives. Steeplechases were held at Forges, a Glebe meadow between Seven Stones and St Annes. There was wrestling, a regatta at Wonwell beach, and Harvest Supper was the highlight of the year.

Kingston had its own brass band and a fine football team and during Queen Victoria's reign a travelling German band came with a performing bear. Barges brought coal up the river and horses and carts fetched it, the animals having to swim out to the boats with the carts floating behind.

Ringmore is another typical, unspoilt South Hams village with a fine church and romantic, cob walled cottages. The Journey's End is an old smugglers' inn where R.C. Sheriff wrote his play of that name with an all male cast which became known world wide after the first world war.

To the east of Ringmore, standing on the west bank of the River Avon is Bigbury where you can see the walls of the ancient farmyard of Bigbury Court, the old manor, which has a fine circular dovecote in the middle of the courtyard. Half a mile away is St Ann's Chapel and the Pickwick Inn which is part of a 14th century chapel. In 1930 when some alterations were taking place a chest containing letters and documents was found in one of the walls. At the time the owners felt no one would want that kind of rubbish and threw them on the bonfire. Who knows what wealth of historic information perished. It is said that one of the upper rooms was used as a meeting place for the Royalists who came here from their various manor houses in the area.

St Ann was a Celtic goddess with a revolting partiality for babies in her diet! Evidence shows that the heads were thrown into wells named after her. At the time the church was legitimising pagan saints by building churches on their religious sites some of which were holy wells.

Aveton Gifford is approached by a long bridge over the marshes, and in the river above is a salmon trap. From the village a four mile long tidal reach begins with a tidal road covered at high tide so there is always an element of excitement and anticipation as you drive along between poles which mark its passage showing the hard road between the mud flats and inlets. This is known locally as 'The Sticks' for an obvious reason. It is wise to make sure you know the tide time before you venture across, the reckless have been known to regret the omission of this knowledge as they stand on the bank watching their car disappear beneath the incoming rush of tide.

Aveton Gifford Church.

BIGBURY BAY
TO THE YEALM

The village of Hope Cove is aptly named as it gave hope to generations of shipwrecked seamen. Once a flourishing settlement it had no estuary so its sons grew up skilled in the handling of boats off and on the beach. Their livelihood at one time came mostly from pilchards, for the whole of Bigbury Bay and particularly the area around Hope Quay was famous for those fish, and then later for the crabs and lobsters which grew to enormous size in the rich waters; sadly now this has almost vanished and in summer the beaches are crowded with sun worshippers so that it would be difficult for the men to launch their boats even if they wished to do so. Alongside fishing in the olden days smuggling was another source of income, mostly of brandy and tobacco - so perhaps in many ways life has not changed all that much although it is the 'furriners' and not the locals now engaged in this practice. Most of the young men who would have grown up to be fishermen like their fathers and grandfathers have had to go to the cities to make a living.

Driving down the hill past Galmpton to outer Hope you are at first a little disappointed as the hills are covered with modern houses, hotels and guest-houses, but the village is divided into two and turning left to drive up the steep hill you look down on Inner Hope with its cob cottages clustered round a small square, caught in a kind of picture book time warp - cottages washed cream, pink and white under thatched roofs. The word cob is a term for a kind of sophisticated clay or mud, a mixture of soil, pebbles, straw, water, cow dung and hair, built up in layers each three feet thick, every layer left to dry before the next one is added, the walls are both warmer in winter and cooler in summer than any modern building but do need their heads and feet kept dry! Here too is the building that once housed the lifeboat which had a 50 years life span, built in 1878 by the Grand Lodge of Freemasons with their emblem showing on the front of the building. Many of the local fishermen were out-standingly heroic in their rescues and received medals on a visit to Buckingham Palace, the boat finished its work when Salcombe received a motorised vessel. At its first launch from Hope on 17th January 1887 it was called to a ship named the 'Hallowe'en' wrecked in Soar Mill Cove, a tea clipper, it spewed the tea over the beach and eventually a 12ft high tea wall was formed. Somehow an opportunist business tycoon in London got wind of this and employed local farmers to cart it to the train for London. That was the last heard of him and the farmers got no pay for their trouble.

The boat was out of use for a period early in the 1920s, back in service between 1926 to 1930, and then retired. Altogether the men of the tiny village saved 64 lives. The history of wrecks in the area would fill several books, but the one still talked of by local people is of the Ramillies, the worst tragedy ever to occur in the area. On 15th February 1760, a 74 gun ship of the line commanded by Captain Taylor, part of Admiral Boscawen's fleet with a crew of 720, left Plymouth earlier in the month for blockade duty off the French coast. On 11th February a south westerly gale, accompanied by driving rain and sleet, caught the ships in open sea. The Ramillies had become detached from the rest of the fleet and was smashed to pieces on Bolt Tail with less than 24 survivors. It seems they discovered, as have so many others since, that what they thought was Rame Head was the then named Island of Burgh in Bigbury Bay and before they could rectify the error they were hopelessly embayed. The sailing master ordered all canvas to be set, under the tremendous strain the mainsail gave way and split from top to bottom, crashing to the deck as the ship struck the rocks. Mountainous seas swept all the men on to the jagged rocks. The Captain of the Marines went off his head and marched up and down, singing. The ship's Bo'sun, who had brought his little son with him, tried to save the child by throwing him towards the shore, only to see him dashed on the rocks. More than 700 men and women died that night at the foot of Bolt Tail, the next day Bigbury Bay was a mass of floating wreckage and bodies. In 1906 a diver visited the spot and found iron canons and a brass wheel.

In 1907 the Jebba suffered the same fate in the same spot but this time everyone was saved by the bosun's chair including the ship's cat, two chimpanzees and a parrot.

During the Second World War Ike Jarvis, one of a large local fishing family, whilst on his way back from pulling crab pots discovered a Flying Fortress bomber which had crashed. The crew were in a dinghy which was slowly sinking and he managed to get them into his boat and take them safely ashore. Jack Jarvis, another member of the same family, was involved with the rescue of the Louis Sheid on 7th December 1939 which was carting a crew of 46 and a cargo of grain. The crew of this boat had seen the Dutch passenger liner Tajandoen sunk by enemy torpedo. The Hope fishermen went to her aid and took on board 62 survivors but by then the Louis Shied herself was stranded and the life boat from Salcombe had to come to her aid. For many years the stark outline of the wreck remained in the bay.

There are many legends of silver and gold ingots, pieces of eight and doubloons and dollars buried beneath the sand of the coves having been washed up from wrecks, and ships' timbers are scattered everywhere. Some years ago some children digging sandcastles on Thurlestone beach found some bodies. These had apparently been there over 200 years and the authorities dug up the remains which were reburied in Galmpton churchyard.

At one time passengers in the East Indiamen coming to London from the Orient and other foreign places, wanting to save time on their journey would be brought ashore at Hope where they could get the chaise to Kingsbridge and from there the coach to Exeter and London. At one time in the 17th century there were about 100 residents in the village, and on occasions dozens of ships used to take shelter for a week or more until a favourable wind sprang up. This meant the sailors came ashore and mixed with the local people, probably telling them tales of all the wonderful places they visited and spending money on provisions brought in from all the surrounding farms.

The Hope and Anchor is a typical fishing village pub so named after the anchor used in times gone by as an extra precaution in a heavy storm if the original one was liable to drag, hence the name. Fishermen will hire you a boat or take you out fishing and there is a family fun week in late August for everyone. There are holiday apartments, cottages and a luxurious hotel with wonderful sea views, and of course guesthouses all of which give a warm welcome. Most romantic of all perhaps, below Bolt Tail which belongs to the National Trust, is a bay with a cave where a noted smuggler, Ralph, used to hide his swag and it is still known as Ralph's Hole.

A mile west of Hope is Thurlestone Rock, the name meaning pierced stone, which it is. The village of Thurlestone again has picture postcard cottages covered with roses and the gardens bright with fuschias and geraniums. There is another beautiful sandy beach here and above the village stands the luxurious Thurlestone Hotel commanding views across the whole of the bay.

It has been in the Grose family since 1895 when Willaim Grose who was a farmer in the Wadebridge area moved his family and stock to Thurlestone. His wife was an excellent cook and she started to do cream teas and other food for visitors. At that time people were starting to come to the area by train, particularly golfers and so the Grose family erected their first sign, 'Thurlestone House. Golfers Accommodated. Picnic Parties Catered For. Terms Moderate'. Soon their reputation for excellence spread and whilst he was Prince of Wales and attending the Royal Naval College at Dartmouth Edward VIII came over for one of their famous cream teas and a game of golf on the small course which has now become well known as being in one of the most beautiful settings in England.

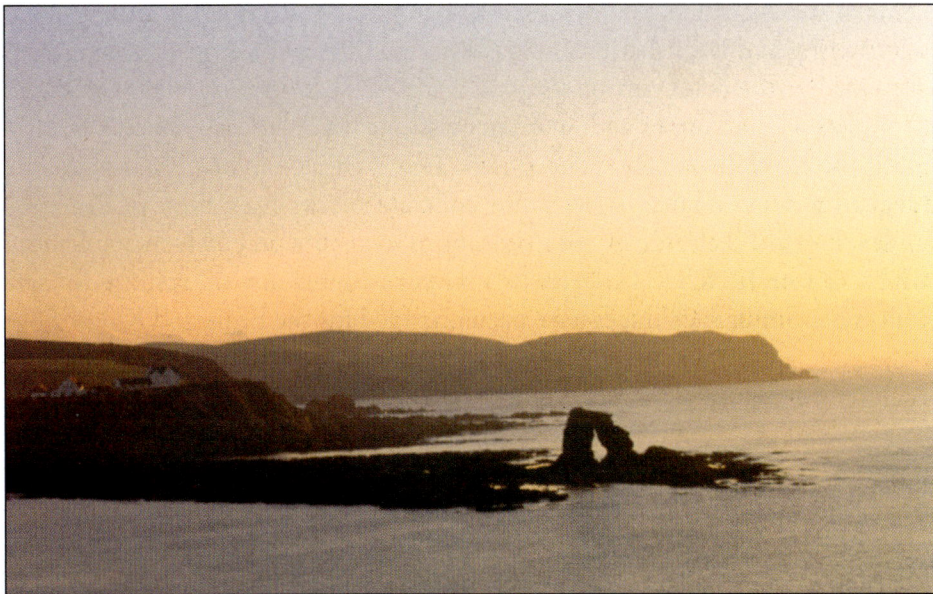

Thurlestone Rock.

The Grose family added more buildings, a fleet of carriages was bought to ferry visitors to and from Kingsbridge station, which in turn became a fleet of cars including a much admired Studebaker. During the war the hotel was taken over by two girls' schools, then commandeered by the marines during which time there was a good deal of damage to the property. With petrol rationing things became difficult but soon the hotel started to flourish again and now offers every facility to the visitor.

Bantham is a mile further west at the mouth of The Avon or Aune as some people call it. Once a hive of industry with sloops and barges in the harbour. At low water its sands are rich with juicy cockles where both grown ups and small boys can be seen searching for these succulent shellfish. Once cargoes of limestone and coal were landed, and corn and potatoes taken away. It even had its own pilot who rowed beyond the sand bar taking ships in and out. He also ran the ferry from Bantham to Bigbury. The Ham is covered with vegetation forming a spit across the mouth of the river and once a Roman camp was said to stand here. Behind is Jenkins' Quay where stands what was once a salmon fisherman's boathouse, now a private dwelling, fish too used to be salted here. The Sloop Inn built in the 16th century was said once to be owned by the smuggler John Widdon and Nat Claverley, a man of the same 'profession' who brought in rum and brandy in the 1700s. Once they even made their own coins or tokens which could be used in Bantham. Today the Inn offers luxury self catering and is a fisherman's paradise. One side of the beach has dangerous currents but the main part offers good water for surfing at the right tide times and there are sand dunes with marram grass; the water is warm and it is an ideal place for children to play. The unsafe area is clearly marked and there are lifeguards in attendance. Two 4 ton concrete blocks have been buried deep under the sand each side of the river mouth to anchor an emergency oil boom which can be stretched between two posts to funnel any oil spillage for safe collection. Similar achorages have been provided for the Erme and Kingsbridge estuary.

Bigbury-on-Sea has a population of between 300 to 400. The coast road used to peter out at Mount Folly Farm into a rough track to the shore. The first houses appeared early in the 20th century, and the main complex of buildings began life as curing cellars for pilchards. Mr Stevens of Modbury converted it into a bus depot and eventually the site included the Tom Crocker Inn in memory of the smuggler from Burgh Island who was shot by a customs man. At one time there had been plans to bring the railway here, but they never materialised.

It was here too that Archibald Nettlefold started up what is now known as Bigbury Golf Club when he built his hotel on Burgh Island, a cup in his name is still played for. He was the originator of the firm known world wide as GKN, maker of screws and other engineering requirements. The Course now is the property of Evans Estates of Cardiff. In 1936 when Archie sold the island he also sold the golf course to 12 members of the club, provided they formed a limited company to run it.

A visit to Burgh Island is a must. Although there is no public right of way to the top of the privately owned island, there is no objection to visitors walking there to visit the huer's hut from where you can see the whole sweep of Bigbury Bay. Landwards you can imagine that once the fields shone with silver covered with the flesh from the pilchards which were sold to the farmers as fertiliser after the oil had been extracted from them in the curing cellars. A huer kept watch for the shoals of pilchards arriving in the Bay, calling out the fishermen to cast their nets. To reach the island is an adventure, for if the tide is high you

Burgh Island.

will need to travel in the unique ferry tractor, specially designed and made in Newton Abbot. It is used to navigate the difficult channel into which the incoming tide makes a pincer like movement so that using small boats as ferries is impossible. The slender link of hard sand at low tide takes a knowledgeable driver to negotiate and it is not advisable to attempt to drive a car across, several have been lost, overcome by the rapidly advancing tide.

The pub on the Island is appropriately called The Pilchard built in the 14th century by monks who grazed their sheep here and used in days past regularly by smugglers. One of these was Tom Crocker as already mentioned, shot by a Custom's Officer and it is said his ghost is a regular visitor to the pub. You can still see the outline of his profile complete with pipe in the stones of the fireplace. At one time the Island was known as St Michael's La Burgh, Island of Burgh, and in the 15th century as Burrough.

The hotel was built in 1929 by Archibald Nettlefold and was frequented by his friends and business associates. It was lavishly decorated and furnished in period style. Today you can still see all this exactly as it was and step back in the 1930s with dances held in keeping with the period, echoes of the famous dance bands which blared out jazz, and 'flappers' from London who swarmed down as guests, many of them in show business for his wife was an opera singer. It had always had some connection with the stage for in the early part of the century George Chigwin known on the variety stage as the White Eyed Kaffir owned the island and built a wooden house which still stands. It also had a casino and was known as the English Monte Carlo. Harry Roy brought down a band from London, there was a floodlit pool with a small island in the middle where the band played during the hot summer nights. In the Ganges Bar Archie installed the stem post from the top gun deck of HMS Ganges, the last sailing vessel commissioned by the British Navy launched in 1821 and eventually broken up in 1929.

During the last war the Ministry of Defence took the island over for a short time. Today as in the past, it offers a 'Great Escape' from the rat race, filled with an atmosphere of magic and enchantment. Agatha Christie wrote two of her books while staying here, 'Evil Under the Sun' and 'Then There were None', originally known as 'Ten Little Niggers'. Kirk Douglas and the Dave Clark Five made films here. Noel Coward was a visitor, The Duke of Windsor and Mrs Simpson took refuge for a holiday, and the Beatles made it their headquarters when they were playing in Plymouth. Little island is connected to the main one by a steep narrow path and is a natural bird sanctuary for herring gulls, cormorants, kittiwakes and other sea birds.

There is no doubting the beauty of the coastline and Burgh Island but unfortunately the deplorable state of the car park and the dilapidated condition of the building complex accompanying it will probably figure larger in visitor's memories. These amenities are crying out for improvements and perhaps future tourists will not be so disappointed. Beyond Bigbury on Sea is Challaborough with a wonderful sandy beach sheltered by rocky promontories and access to a fine coastal path. Although very small it is now a popular beach resort with hundreds of caravans lining the sides of the valley. At one time all its provisions had to come by sea because travel from inland was so difficult, but now it is easily accessible and a perfect holiday centre from which to explore this part of the South Hams.

The Ferry Tractor.

The Erme Estuary.

Cliffs west of Bigbury.

Mothecombe first referred to in the early 13th century, stands near the mouth of the River Erme and is privately owned, although public access to the beach and estuary is allowed on Wednesdays and at weekends. Flete was a huge Saxon estate, once the home of Lord Mildmay of Flete known to all Devonians for his prowess in the horse racing world. Sadly he drowned when swimming from the beach, probably as the result of cramp brought on by an early riding accident to his neck. He, in company with Peter Cazalet, the racehorse trainer, introduced both the Queen Mother and her daughter to the joys of National Hunt Racing.

In May 1990 the estuary here and Mothecombe itself, were threatened when much of Bigbury Bay became awash with crude oil from the Liberian registered tanker Rose Bay, when it collided with the trawler Dionne Marie from Brixham. An 80 square mile slick threatened the whole area as 1100 tons of crude oil poured out and booms had to be set up across the mouth of the river. It took an army of workmen and much ariel spraying of oil dispersants before the area resumed a semblance of its natural beauty.

Holbeton village is set back a little from the wooded shores of the estuary, the banks of which are lined with country houses such as Flete. Here are good pubs with home cooking, fish being a speciality, one has a carvery and their own brewery in the garden.

Noss Mayo and Newton Ferrers lie opposite each other on a creek of the beautiful wooded estuary of the Yealm. Since the 1930s they have been referred to as Newton and Noss, although remaining separate church parishes. Newton Ferrers has somewhat unfairly been called the poor man's Salcombe, but it is a glorious spot with a character quite its own. Both these villages are a little isolated but that is part of their charm. The Yealm estuary is a haven for artists and yachtsmen with pretty waterside cottages once the homes of fishermen, although fishing boats are no longer part of the landscape.

Fishing provided a good livelihood for the coastal dwellers of the South Hams for hundreds of years. At the turn of the century, Newton Ferrers and Noss Mayo supported a fleet of 30 crabbers, and the villages depended on them for much of their economic activity. The pilchard which once were plentiful have disappeared; bass have been fished by commercial boats instead of individual anglers; hand-lining for mackerel has been superseded, as have so many sustainable fishing methods, by the fearsome ravages of modern trawlers. Indiscriminate in what they collect, with no capacity to distinguish species, age, maturity, or size, they threaten the survival of the fish stocks in a way which larger mesh, smaller size nets, or individual small boat fishing methods never did. The decline of the fishing villages bears witness to the practically non-existent environmental management of our fish stocks during the last 50 years. Now they rely on tourism for their income, the visitors coming to look at the relics left by an industry which once supplied a handsome income as well as healthy food. It is not the fault of the fishermen. Like the villagers of old Hallsands, they warned what was happening. Like the villagers of old Hallsands, they were ignored. We are not quite at the point of disaster for all species, though some are under very serious threat of never being able to recover. Unless some dramatic action is taken very soon, fish will become but a memory for most people, the sections about cooking it in recipe books as quaint and irrelevant to most of us as Mrs. Beeton's often quoted recipe for Jugged Hare. A fine commentary on the foresight and intelligence of a nation, to exterminate one of the main components of the dish which half the world thinks we live on - fish and chips. (The other half, of course, know we live on bacon and eggs).

Noss Mayo.

Newton Ferrers with its steep hills and woodlands that flank the riverbank is especially popular with yachtsmen during the summer as it has its sheltered creek. There are three pubs all within a stone's throw of the water.

Equally beautiful is Noss Mayo offering first class catering facilities and a converted barn to rent. From here a path leads around a spectacular piece of coastline called Warren Point where butterflies abound and narrow, sheep trodden paths wind down to the sea. Walking enthusiasts could take the ferry across the river and take the path leading to the mouth and along the coast to the parish of Wembury with its little church of St Werburgh standing on the cliff at the junction of several of the parish footpaths, well worth a visit. It has stood on this wild piece of coast since the 14th century, the date of the tower, the rest of the building is 15th century. In 1683 Sir Warwick Hele built the almshouses with a little chapel in the centre where services were held and where once people queued along the lane past the building to attend. The ancestors of John Galsworthy of Forsythe Saga fame came from here and he describes the church in 'Swan Song'. He could trace his ancestors back to the 12th century who farmed in this parish. Offshore is the Great Mewstone, a rock like a right angled triangle where people have lived in the past. Many secluded coves around here can only be reached on foot, on Wembury Point stands HMS Cambridge, the gunnery training establishment. In the area there are cottages to rent, holiday cabins to hire in a peaceful wooded valley with a shop; laundrette and stables only 500 metres from the beach. There is a newly opened Marine Visitor Centre giving a glimpse of rare underwater wildlife. Not far away near Yealmpton is the famous Shire Horse Centre, and in the village itself, Old Mother Hubbard's Cottage from the nursery rhyme by Sarah Martin - surely the South Hams has something for everyone.

THE HENLEY HOTEL

Folly Hill. Bigbury-on-Sea. Kingsbridge. **Tel: 01548 810240**

Commanding one of the most spectacular views of Devon, this small friendly cottage hotel overlooks the Avon estuary, Burgh Island and Bigbury Bay! J.W. Turner was believed to have sat in the garden to create his picture of the bay and Longstone Rock. There are eight bedrooms, all having telephone, colour T.V. with satellite, radio and tea/coffee making facilities. Families are well catered for and can include pets. Children particularly welcome. The hotel has a fine reputation for good food, and much use is made of the fresh local produce. Most major credit cards are accepted. AA 1 Star, English Tourist Board Commended and member of LOGIS of Great Britain

THE FORTESCUE

UNION STREET. SALCOMBE. **Telephone: (01548) 842868**

What a lovely Devon inn - and what a magic setting. The Fortescue is the real village inn; frequented by the locals including the crew of the famous Salcombe Lifeboat based just 50 yards down the road. Open all day, from 11.00 a.m. to 11.00 p.m. this character inn has Real Ales, good food and a fine welcome, winter and summer. Daily specials on the blackboard feature local fish including turbot, brill, sole and - of course - Salcombe crabs! Your hosts are Peter and Christine Milton who also run the wine shop and off-licence across the road.

THURLESTONE HOTEL

THURLESTONE VILLAGE. SOUTH DEVON.
Telephone: 01548 560382

Celebrating its centenary in 1996, the Thurlestone Hotel has been owned and run by the Grose family since 1896. It is a truly magnificent four-star establishment which has offered a very special standard of elegance, comfort and service, with each generation of the Grose family adding some special facet to the identity that has made the hotel a favourite with families that come here year after year - as did their parents and grandparents before them! Indoor and outdoor heated swimming pools; solarium and sauna, Jacuzzi and gymnasium, here are facilities to be enjoyed and appreciated, for they are of the highest quality. The sixty eight bedrooms are furnished and equipped to the standards you would expect form this 'world-class' hotel.

The restaurant is renowned, and the 24 hour room service equals - if not exceeds - the best London has to offer. There are a limited numer of family rooms where children are accommodated free of charge (12 years old and under), Call for details. There is a new Clarins Beauty Salon, and for golfing enthusiasts a 50% concession has been negotiated with Bigbury Golf Club. The hotel also offers tennis coaching, golf tuition, in-house launderette for guests (in addition to full laundry and valet service) and every other amenity expected of an hotel of this calibre. Visa/Mastercard accepted.

RAC/AA Four Star • Five Crowns Highly Commended
Egon Ronay Recommended

MEMBER OF THE
SOUTH HAMS FOOD &
DRINK ASSOCIATION

The PORT LIGHT HOTEL

- *Restaurant and Inn* -

BOLBERRY. NR. SALCOMBE. **TEL: (01548) 561384**

The seascape from this friendly small hotel is amazing - there's no other word for it. 180 degrees of sea and sky - and you can almost see France! It was once an R.A.F. radar station, perched high on the cliffs just a stone's throw away from Hope Cove, with spectacular sunsets over Bigbury Bay. The food is all home-cooked, and proprietor Sean Hassall and his wife Sonya care for every aspect of the comfort and happiness of guests. There are six en suite rooms, all with colour television and tea/coffee making facilities, and the larger de-luxe rooms also have trouser press, hairdryers etc. Purpose built children's play area, and fabulous walks in every direction! The prices are most reasonable, there is a children's menu too, and the food is quite excellent using local suppliers and selecting the very best of the season's fare. The Hotel is open for Christmas and New Year, but then closes for the rest of January. Devon Cream Teas are also served from 3.30 p.m. to 5.00 p.m. at weekends during 'the season'. Visa/Mastercard.

IVYBRIDGE

Ivybridge is unquestionably the gateway to Dartmoor, the start or finish of the Two Moors Way, a hundred mile trail which crosses Dartmoor and Exmoor.

In 1817 the population was 477, in 1954 the great historian W.G. Hoskins referred to it "Ivybridge is now a small market town," but quoted no population figures saying he often found these unreliable.

How times have changed for in 1994 the population was approx 10,000 and it could be described as a perfect example or microcosm of a Devon village becoming a thriving town, fairly typical of many in the South Hams today.

Ivy Bridge first appears in 1280 AD taking its name from the ancient bridge over the River Erme - a river obviously anxious to reach the sea as it rushed

down the valley to the town. The bridge was only wide enough for pack horses and riders, but with the coming of the 20th century and with Plymouth growing rapidly the bridge was widened to accommodate the great increase in traffic.

Back in the 16th century there was insurrection, discontent and violence; in 1549 the owner of a tin mill, on the Harford side of the river, John Bury, was a ringleader of a Rebellion known as the Prayer Book Rebellion which involved

Archbishop Cranmer's revision, and he was hanged at Tyburn in 1550.

At the time of the Armada in 1588 Ivybridge consisted of two dwelling houses, a corn mill and an edger mill (of tools) standing in 180 acres of arable land. By the 17th century the little community of manor tenants began to show signs of becoming a village, the inhabitants living by agriculture, and working in the woollen industry. There had been a tucking mill at Harford as early as 1555.

In 1620 William Hunwill built a fulling mill next to the corn mill with whom he shared the leat water; he also built three houses, and others started to spring up below the bridge on the west bank of the river - a blacksmith, joiner, weaver and so on. The joiner built himself a house on land now occupied by the Erme Constitutional Club. In other words Ivybridge was fast becoming a typical self-supporting Devon village with Plympton market only six miles away, and according to Risdon the road through Ivybridge had become "A great thoroughfare."

In 1692 Ivybridge was sold to John Rogers, a merchant from Plymouth for £3,500 and was held by that family until 1895. The sale came through William Drake who was related to Sir Francis Drake, and another famous man, Sir Joshua Reynolds had a friend who lived in the mansion known as Highlands where he kept his unique collection of prints, drawings and bronzes now in Plymouth Art Gallery.

One of the most famous products of the town is paper, mostly because of the purity of the water. Stowford Paper Mill was built in 1787 by William Dunsterville, a Plymouth miller who bought Stowford Barton and built a large paper mill, still operating today. Others were built further down the river and in 1849 John Allen, a Plymouth malster, bought the mills as a speculative enterprise. During the 1860s he added up to date machinery so the mills went from strength to strength, employing more than 200 people. For many years all the paper for postage stamps was made here. Eventually the mills passed to Wiggins Teape in 1930 and in 1991 they merged with a French firm to become Arjo Wiggins Fine Paper Ltd.

In the 19th century roads were turnpiked and a toll exacted. It took more than 25 years from these first being installed before the full effect was seen in Ivybridge. These included a spiked barrier being swung across to ward off attack from mounted riders who resented being held up to pay dues, and took exception to the wheeled traffic which caused their horses to shy and covered their clothes with mud. There was also much argument over the list of exemptions from toll which included all mail, carts carrying road repairing material, farm carts and horses going to pasture or water. Much cheating and smuggling resulted.

In 1787 a new inn was built, The London Inn, on the east side of the river. It soon gained a reputation for being one of the most comfortable inns in the south west, sadly now no more, it was bought by the South Hams District Council in 1992 to be converted into flats and offices.

To return to the Rogers family, they were now determined to make Ivybridge a pleasant place in which to live and in 1777 Sir Frederick granted people small plots of land on which to build. In 1793 he introduced a cattle market where Ivybridge Motors now stands. This was intended to be a monthly affair, but only took place a couple of times. He then built a racecourse on Henlake Down with a meeting held each year on a Monday in either May, June or July, until the year 1797 in which he died. Meanwhile he had agreed with Christopher Lethbridge for a new inn, to be the Rogers Arms, now Grosvenor House.

In 1813 it seems obtaining water became a problem for some of the mills and a leat was cut taking water from the Erme at a weir in Henlake Down Woods. This was carried out at Sir John Roger's expense. In 1832 Sir John allowed a certain John Seldon to license his house by the river and this became the Kings Arms, now the Exchange. Manor Court dinners were held here for the tenants, but unfortunately on leaving the Inn customers had difficulty in avoiding the open leat which ran in front of the building.

In 1848 the South Devon Railway reached Plymouth and Ivybridge got a station. In his book 'Small Talk at Wreyland' Cecil Torr gives a picture of what went on when the railway in Devon was being built. "The navvies (many were Irish) made things unpleasant here while the line was building ... a pretty row there was, drunk altogether and fighting, one couple fought in the meadows for an hour and got badly served." This would have been in his own area of Lustleigh, but it seemed to occur universally. There were many complaints that the sparks from the engines would set light to thatched roofs and mothers shut there daughters safely indoors for fear they would be ravished. Landslips were a menace as the cuttings passed through the Devon hills, much as when, years later, the motorways were cut. However once the rail was established it became a popular method of transport and the Royal family used Ivybridge station to visit nearby Flete.

In 1959 it was closed to passenger traffic but opened again in 1994. The station is being promoted as a park and ride for Plymouth. In 1859 Ivybridge Board School opened — in 1874 the tollhouse in Cole Lane was sold and in 1894 Ivybridge Urban District Council was formed. This was disbanded in 1935. In 1900 the Union Mills were taken over by Henry James Fice Lee and at this time the post office was in its original site at the Sunnyside Guest House. In 1928 Local authority housing was built in Mill Meadow and in 1931 the tollhouse in Cole Lane was demolished.

Life went on with more building of houses and schools, in 1962 the population was 1775 and it officially became a town in 1977 with a council and mayor. There followed the not uncommon history of plans and counter plans for development along with delays and changes. In 1987 the South Dartmoor Leisure Centre opened, and in 1988 the new shopping centre on the site of Ivybridge Corn Mills also opened. There is a Tourist Information Centre, a Chamber of Trade and a Federation of small businesses. In their County Guide to Devon, Shire Publications said in 1989 "Ivybridge has expanded as a dormitory town to Plymouth and now it is an example of mushroom growth, said to be the fastest growing town in England, it is in commuter land, its green slopes now covered in housing estates." Until 1973 people travelling to Plymouth cursed the long and winding main street, the new A38 bypass cured this.

The Leisure Centre is one of the best of its kind in the area with indoor and outdoor pools, specially popular with parents of young children because there are areas of shallow water. Indoor facilities include squash, badminton, table tennis, a fully equipped multi fitness suite and a fast tanning sunbed. A health and fitness suite offers the best range of training equipment to suit all levels of interest, ability and age from the absolute beginner to the more accomplished keep-fitter. There are qualified staff to give expert information.

There is a large selection of club activities including martial arts, netball, junior football, aerobics and gymnastics; a Riverside Bar and the Riverside Suite provides a venue for various entertainments.

The Tourist Information Centre is open six days a week, seven in summer with every type of information available including a local bed booking service.

Eating out is one of the main pleasures of a holiday and in Ivybridge there is a wide selection ranging from snacks to full meals and cream teas. The shopping centre in the old part of the town is easily reached from the car park across the wooden bridge over the river. There are guided walks on Dartmoor, easy trail leaflets are available and the many footpaths are well signed all over the South

Hams.

In spite of the growth that has occurred, some things don't change and Ivybridge still straddles the river Erme, and Western Beacon still overlooks the town and the magnificent and romantic valley. With riverside, woodland and moorland walks, leisure facilities and good shopping, Ivybridge is an ideal place in which to base your holiday, and you can learn much more about it by following the Town Trail from the Tourist Information Centre with one of the special leaflets. As you walk through the town you will notice it seems full of young, cheerful people who will give you a warm welcome.

Of course it must be remembered that there is enormous interest to be found also in the surrounding countryside. Cornwood with its china clay workings is a good finishing point for a moorland walk or drive. Ermington is a Saxon plan village overlooking the Erme valley with a leaning church spire, twisting and turning rather like a jester's cap, said to be the result of the wedding of a beautiful lady called Miss Bulteel - when she reached the church door the tower was overcome by her beauty that it bowed low to look at her and couldn't straighten up!

Many villages in the area are worth a visit, too numerous to detail here, but South Brent just off the A38 as you travel west from Ivybridge is another base for walkers to such places as the Avon Dam reservoir. From here too the original Primrose Line started which ran to Kingsbridge, so named because of the great carpet of flowers that lined the banks along the track in spring. The line, 12^1/$_2$ miles long was opened in 1893. It had 48 wrought iron bridges, crossed the river Avon in ten places and had a tunnel 660 yards long at Sorley, part of which can still be seen at the Farm and Craft Centre where there are also workshops and animals to be seen. The last train, suitably garlanded ran along the rails and ended the life of the Primrose Line at the early age of 70. You can still see where it ran on the Ordnance Survey map, but floods have largely eliminated the primroses.

For golfers there is Wrangaton Golf Club with an 18 hole combined moorland and parkland course 6041 yards long, with a resident professional and a good clubhouse. The course was literally carved out of gorse and bracken by local golfing pioneers, first established in 1895 as a 9 hole moorland course on relatively level ground at the foot of Ugborough Beacon. Ninety three years later 50 acres of adjoining farmland were bought for development into 9 parkland holes designed by the top British golf course architect, Donald Steel, and opened for play in April 1991, offering a unique and interesting blend of golf combining the natural ruggedness of the moor with the gentler features of parkland.

Salmon, trout and sea trout can be caught in the river Erme or you can visit a trout farm in the area.

Mention must be made of Buckfast Abbey, founded in 1018 by Benedictine monks; a victim of the Dissolution, then in 1907 as the result of a vision in which he was told to rebuild the Abbey, a young monk started his life's work with just a handful of helpers and by 1938 the Abbey had been rebuilt. The monks established their industry in their world famous tonic wine, honey from their apiary and a farm. They receive half a million visitors a year to see the Abbey and visit the tea rooms, shops, and exhibitions.

The Abbey still remains a spiritual centre with daily services and retains an extraordinary tranquillity if for a little while you want to relax and be quiet.

Endsleigh Garden Centre

IVYBRIDGE. DEVON. Telephone: (01752) 892254

One of Devon's largest and most popular garden centres, Endsleigh covers over 8 acres with more than 40,00 square feet under cover. There is a gift shop, and book section, pet shop and mountain bike centre as well as a children's play area and very high quality tea shop/restaurant which has local produce and preserves including home-made cakes and biscuits. As members of the HTA and GCA, Endsleigh has a fine reputation for a superb selection of plants, trees, houseplants and shrubs as well as aquatics, floristry and garden equipment.

Open throughout the year, the centre provides every attraction for a day out for the family, and has been featured on radio and television as well as in the national press. Parking for 500+ cars, with separate exhibitions displaying conservatories and garden sheds/summer houses, garden furniture, swimming pools, landscaping and design, lawnmowers, and other equiment.

The Ship Inn

UGBOROUGH. NR. IVYBRIDGE. DEVON. **Telephone: (01752) 892565**

This delightful inn has earned a most remarkable reputation for food. Not only that, but the prices are by any standards, reasonable, with lunch at around £5 to £6 and dinner at under £12. The lunch menu features such dishes as venison, seafood lasagne, Breton style fish stew served with garlic bread, braised oxtails and roast beef with Yorkshire pudding - to mention but a few! All home-made, fresh local produce (wherever possible). Fish is a speciality, and the evening menu features a dish of monkfish scallops and mussels in a turmeric, oregano and tomato sauce with white wine and cream. Real Ales and a first class selection of wines including French, German, Spanish, Italian and New World selections - again at very sensible prices. No credit cards - but at these prices that makes sense. Plenty of parking in the lovely village square *(No jukebox or one-armed bandits)!*

The Anchor Inn

UGBOROUGH. DEVON. Telephone: (01752) 892283

The Anchor Inn dates back to 1392. Tucked away in this unspoiled village, it remains much as it might have been a century or more ago. The timbered inn has expanded into adjoining cottages and now offers accommodation in the form of five en suite 'cabins' (modernised, but original Devon cottages). There is a fine restaurant offering a first-rate a la carte menu and blackboard daily 'specials', and local game is much in demand. Quail in apricots and brandy, pheasant with Seville oranges and sherry vie for your attention with fresh lobster … and even bison and ostrich steaks! Real Ales and a fine atmosphere. Open every day. Last orders 10.00 p.m. Visa & Mastercard welcome.

The Church House Inn

RATTERY. NR. SOUTH BRENT. S. DEVON
Telephone: 01364 642220

This remarkable inn is the oldest in Devon.... Monks lived here when they were building the church - in 1028 AD, and the landlord has a recorded list of his predecessors dating back to 1660. The inn is preserved as 'An Ancient Monument of Special Architectural and Historic interest' and when you enter, you can see why. Great open fireplaces with crackling log fires in winter, and a massive oak screen and beams create a feeling of times past as nothing else could. This is a true family run inn, and has received many accolades from top guides, and been featured on television.

The food is excellent. Bar meals - everything is home-cooked - and these feature steak & kidney pie, chicken wensleydale, steaks (up to 16oz), gammon and many, many more. There are also blackboard specials of the day offering guinea fowl with a redcurrant and raspberry sauce with port, turkey escallops with blackberry and cranberry sauce and many other delights. There is a fine wine list; over 60 carefully selected varieties, and as well as Real Ales, the inn has 40 single malt whiskies to choose from! I could happily move in here!

THE SOUTH DEVON COASTAL PATH

(SOUTH HAMS SECTION)

The South Devon Coast Path is part of the longest, and arguably the loveliest and most exciting, footpath in the United Kingdom. An official Long Distance Trail, the South West Coastal Path runs from Minehead in Somerset, round the entire South West peninsula to Poole, in Dorset. It travels some of the most beautiful coastline in the world and whether you tackle it with the firm intention of walking every inch of the 600 plus miles, or simply stroll odd stretches of it bit by bit as a pleasant way of spending time on a lovely day, you are sure to find it offers you something new at every turn.

The section of the South Devon Coast Path which runs along the coastline of the South Hams offers some of the most stimulating walks, with focuses of interest from the natural world, through evidence of the long established human population of the area, to busy and historically built environments. It is the landfall of many migrating species of birds and butterflies, as well as home to a wide variety of wildlife. There will be many sources of pleasure as even a section you know well and walk regularly will offer you new flowers, new birds, or a new colour scheme, as the seasons change.

Walking is excellent exercise for the eye, the brain and the body, which is perhaps why people of widely varied backgrounds and ages find it so satisfying. There are sections of the coastal path which can be undertaken as a circular walk from a car park, or a local bus service, and are ideal for the casual potterer out for a stroll to enjoy the view. Other sections are steep and slippery, into the teeth of the wind more often than not, and require more serious preparation, even in summer. A young family, a group of retired friends, teenagers on expeditions, serious walkers from home and abroad, you will meet them all as you walk, and each will take away a different experience from your own.

There are many sources of information about the coastal path. If you are staying in the area, or have recently moved in, talk to the people you meet. Often a hotel will be experienced in ferrying people to the start of a walk, or the bed and breakfast hostess will have details of taxis, tide tables, and ferries to allow you to plan your own foray along the coast. A chat in the pub will flush out the favourite walks of the locals, and they will enthusiastically steer you to follow their footsteps. You may find the local library has books, but beware relying too heavily on any that are more than a year or two old, because things change.

A jointly funded initiative of the local councils and the Countryside Commission has established the Heritage Coast Service, and the rangers engaged by the Service help to ensure the maintenance of the path and the provision of information about it. They arrange talks and events, such as Christmas tree planting on the dunes - not as outrageous as it sounds, since these are the trees discarded after Christmas, which are buried in such a way as to help bind the sand together, to prevent further erosion.

You will find in the bookshops and some local outlets, excellent guides based on detailed Ordnance Survey maps, or aerial photographs, and of course, pub and accommodation guides which are useful for planning longer expeditions along the path. All or any are a good investment in order to plan your journey to give you the most enjoyment. Perhaps the best value, simple but packed with good practical information as well as details of interesting features, are the packs of leaflets, arranged in sets of five day walks, published by the Heritage Coast Service. These are available from many local sources, principally the Tourist Information Centre, and some post offices, hotels and pubs.

Enticed by the photographs of remote headlands such as Start Point, with its lighthouse; the bustling sailing centres of Newton Ferrers and Salcombe; the historic town of Dartmouth, and the magical pull of an island, you will find it hard to decide where to begin. How long a walk do you fancy? (How fit are you, might be a good question). How difficult should it be? Do you have one, or even two cars available to you, to leave at either end of the walk, or do you need to be near public transport? What time of year will this particular walk be at its best?

Not an easy question. A simple, level stretch of coast can become a wild and challenging environment with the addition of a gale and driving rain, and these are by no means confined to the winter months! You can find yourself enveloped in sea mist, utterly isolated from sound and sight, after starting out on a fine summer morning. On the other hand, winter can bring flocks of migrating birds to add to the interest of a sunny, crisp and breathtaking clear days, as well as the possibility of having long stretches of the walk to yourself. Whenever you walk, don't forget that you will be visiting some of the remotest areas of the county. Wear the right clothing. Always carry a waterproof. In winter, you need a hat to help you to keep warm. 25% of your body's heat is lost through you head. When you get too hot on an energetic climb, simply take off your hat and you will adjust your temperature without the need for shedding your back-pack, a tedious process even if it only contains your sandwiches and a box of plasters. In summer, you need a hat with a brim to shield you from sunburn and glare. The dangers of exposure to strong sunlight are well known these days, and by the sea the sun's strength is increased by the reflection off the water. Remember that even on a dull day the sun can burn and cause problems which will ruin your holiday.

Strong, comfortable footwear is essential. If you have a trusted pair of boots, then you will no doubt choose to wear them. If you wear good trainers, you will be fine on most of the path. You will encounter mud, rock, slippery patches and steep ones, sand and roads at different points and times of the year. Bare feet are essential for wading the one or two points where it is appropriate. A small towel will allow you to replace your shoes without them rubbing, as wet socks can. Also, you are sure to be tempted by some of the delightful coves you will visit, so being equipped for paddling or swimming is a good idea. Never swim off headlands, where strong currents are dangerous.

If you like wearing shorts in summer, you should not encounter difficulties along most of the path, but longish socks are certainly desirable for the parts where sharp, stinging or spiky bits reach out to grab ankles. Sun protection cream is also essential, or you can end up very sore.

Be sensible. Some people feel that any planning robs a day of its spontaneity, but surely it is better to give some thought beforehand to the basics, so that an obvious disaster can be avoided? Think ahead. About footwear, clothing, the weather and food. Are you aiming for a pub where you will have lunch? Are you planning a walk which involves a ferry crossing? Are you intending to catch the bus back? Are you sure they are all open in January?

A small first aid kit can be welcome - some plasters for blistered feet; anti-histamine cream for nettle or insect stings; high factor sun protection cream as mentioned previously, a small pair of scissors; a pair of tweezers; (amazing how often splinters and broken nails need attention); even an elastic knee support, which takes up very little room, but makes life much more comfortable if you have a dodgy knee joint.

Leave a note in the car saying how many there are in your party, where you were heading for, and what time you left. True, car thieves will then know how long they have to raid your vehicle. But it doesn't take them long to break in, and they will get in anyway if they have decided to. You will not have left anything valuable for them to be tempted by, anyway, will you? It is an unfortunate fact of life that car thieves operate throughout the holiday areas, particularly in car parks frequented by walkers. Never take anything in the car that you are not either intending to carry with you when you walk, or are prepared to lose.

If you have booked ahead for a meal or accommodation and change your plans, please tell the person who is expecting you. Otherwise, they may alert the emergency services that you are overdue. This is not simply an embarrassment and a waste of their resources, but can become a disaster for someone else who really needs their services.

Remember that in the South West, 999 the emergency number, connects you not only to the Police, Fire and Ambulance Services, but also to the Coastguard. It is always possible that you were the only person to see a windsurfer or child on an inflatable swept out to sea, or the flare from a boat in difficulties. If in doubt, report it. Then you can hope that one day, if ever you or your family need help, someone else will do the same.

You will be walking spectacular countryside. If you have a light pair of binoculars, they will add to your pleasure, and a camera is something you will regret leaving at home. On the other hand, extra weight on a longish walk is not something you want. A waterproof will also keep out the wind, so you can leave out that extra sweater. A well-fitting rucksack is the most convenient way to carry things, however small it may be, and is desirable even for the shortest and leveliest of walks. That plastic carrier bag will drive you mad and unbalance you, making walking difficult. Ask a friend, or the landlady, if you may borrow one, if you do not have one. And do persuade the smallest member of the party that Teddy will hate the walk and would be much happier keeping an eye on home base, otherwise you know who will end up carrying him. It is, incidentally, amazing how far even small children can walk, and how much they can enjoy it, so think twice before leaving them at home. If you take your dog with you, also take water, and something for him to drink out of. Dogs are drawn to the sea, but it makes their coats sticky and itchy, and if they drink seawater, the salt will make them dehydrated, and potentially very sick. You should keep your dog under control at all times, not least because an enthusiastic welcome from a bouncy dog may spell trouble for a small child overbalancing on a cliff path.

The land you walk through all belongs to someone. The National Trust owns quite a large area, but this is leased to farmers, whose stock must be respected. The footpath is well marked, with signposts carrying the acorn symbol of the Heritage Coast Service, and the yellow arrows which indicate footpaths, (blue for bridleways). You should keep to the right of way at all times.

You will find that most Guides give details of car parks, railway stations, and convenient towns and villages. You may need current information about train services, bus timetables, tides, and ferry services. The Tourist Information Centre will supply all these things, and the Heritage Coast Service leaflets give details of where to find all relevant telephone numbers, including taxis which can take you to the start of the walk. If you leave your car where you intend to finish, it gives you more flexibility over timing, to linger along the way.

Depending on which way you are walking, the path enters or leaves the South Hams just outside Plymouth, at Fort Bovisand. For this short guide we shall assume you intend walking eastwards, with the prevailing wind behind. The Fort is now occupied by an international Diving School, and you can see the small harbour which they use. It was a gun battery, and is one of the 'Palmerston Falls', built by the Victorian Prime Minister as part of the defences of Plymouth. You will see more, on both sides of the Sound. Along this stretch of coast you will encounter many reminders of the military importance of this splendid harbour. First and Second World War gun emplacements crown the headlands, and the path goes both ways round H.M.S. Cambridge, the Royal

Navy Gunnery School at Wembury Point, to allow for times when the guns are being fired. Please take great care in this area! Read all notices, do what they say, and take careful note if the red warning flags are flying - your life could depend on it. The panorama of Plymouth Sound with Drake's Island and the Breakwater changes as you round the cliffs to fine views of Wembury Bay and beyond.

The next major point is the Yealm estuary. If you are continuing your walk, at Warren Point you will need to arrange for a boat to take you across. There is no ferry service. If you break your walk, and start again at Noss Mayo, you avoid this problem. The section from here to the Erme estuary skirts some major landed estates of the past and present, and you will at one point walk part of the 9-mile drive Lord Revelstoke had built so that his guests (who included Queen Victoria) could enjoy the spectacular countryside in some comfort. Ruined summer houses feature, a reminder of elegant living in times past. Across the Erme, only fordable at low tide in reasonable weather, but with the crossing point clearly marked, enjoy the view as you head for Beacon Point, one of the chain of beacons erected to warn of imminent danger of invasion by the Spanish in the sixteenth century. There are distractions along this length of the Path, in the form of diversions to Kingston and Ringmore, with their pretty houses and ancient pubs. The slate cliffs lead on to the prospect of Burgh ('Burr') Island, set at the mouth of the Avon, with another potential diversion to visit the Island, full of history both ancient and more recent, from a fourteenth century inn, to the hotel Agatha Christie and many more other famous people stayed in its fashionable heyday. You can wade to the Island, or even walk dry-shod in certain conditions, or you may take the unique sea-tractor across. If you are out of season for the Avon ferry, a detour via Aveton Gifford, its tidal road full of interest in itself, will be necessary.

At the mouth of the Avon, evidence of occupation soon after the Romans left has been found. More spectacular views of Burgh Island can be enjoyed after the next climb, then the Path passes the well known golf course at Thurlestone. Another village detour is possible, with more thatched cottages and an ancient Inn to entice you away from the path.

One of the country's important wildlife sites is crossed by the wooden bridge at South Milton Ley, where the wetland habitat attracts resident and migrating birds to the reedbeds. This walk will please wildlife enthusiasts, with its wildflowers, butterflies and birds. Passing Thurlestone Rock, the distinctive arched rock just off this particularly rugged run of coast, you will come to another Beacon Point. There are several recurring names along the Path, the same name reflecting the existence of a similar feature, in this case a warning of impending invasion in Elizabethan times. Warren Point is another. The warrens are reminders of the days when rabbits were farmed, and the name occurs all over the country, from the coast to Dartmoor. You will also find many offshore rocks called the Mew Stone, from the old name for the seagulls who nest there.

On to the twin villages of Inner and Outer Hope. Pause to explore the history of this fishing and smuggling centre. The Lifeboat Station is justly famous, though the lifeboat itself was last stationed here over 60 years ago.

Thurlestone Church had in former times a firepan in the tower to warn sailors of the nearness of the coast, an early form of lighthouse. There are wrecks to be seen even now, evidence that even in our days of navigational aids and lighthouses, ships are vulnerable to the hidden, greedy rocks. The locals used these terrors to supplement their meagre income, by lighting fires to mislead ships, attracting them into the rocks, and waiting to steal whatever was washed ashore. Some took rewards for helping 'save' those off the ships. Some simply murdered the survivors. It is hard to imagine how people whose own lives revolved around the dangerous rhythms of a treacherous sea could possibly be drawn into this ghastly way of making money, but it went on for many years.

The 7 miles or so which take you from Hope to Salcombe traverse the dramatic landscape of Bolt Tail and Bolt Head. The views are spectacular. Skirting the Iron Age fort (over 2,000 years old), you will go on past the Decca Navigation radio masts, down to sandy Soar Mill Cove, up on to Bolt Head, until the Salcombe estuary opens before you, Prawle Point beckoning on its far side.

Salcombe, and East Portlemouth on its opposite bank, have a long and fascinating history wound around the sea and seafaring. Now a sailing resort, Salcombe attracts many summer visitors, and the pressure on the local environment is considerable. You can cross the estuary all year round by the ferry.

The quiet village of East Portlemouth has been eclipsed by its neighbour, but was in mediaeval times much the larger. Through the wooded area and on. Early field systems lie to the landward of the path as you head towards the 'pig' rocks, Pig's Nose, Ham Stone and Gammon Head. The path winds up and down round inviting coves, some accessible, to Prawle ('lookout') Point, the southernmost part of Devon. There is good bird spotting to be done on this walk, and also many wildflowers.

Past Prawle Point, note the curious sight of earlier sea cliffs, relics of the ages when the ice locked up water, then melted and raised the sea levels, before once again freezing at the Poles to leave these former fringes of the sea stranded. Lannacombe beach and Mattiscombe Sand will bring you to the rugged headland of Start Point, with its lighthouse, now unmanned and closed to the public. This craggy outcrop has witnessed the end of many vessels over the years, some not so long ago.

Onto a road for a while, towards Hallsands, Beesands and Torcross. The environment of this area, both marine and landward, is very special. The ruined village of Hallsands stands as a warning of what man's interference with established environments can do. The freshwater lakes of Widdicombe Ley and Slapton Ley offer a diversity of wildlife, the latter important on a national scale. Pause to investigate the nature trail, and the tank memorial to those lost in the Normandy Landings of 1944.

From here to Dartmouth, the Path involves some road walking, and leaves the coastal fringe. Dartmouth warrants more than a simple 'passing-through' on any schedule, and whether you stay during a longer expedition on the Coastal Path, or visit it specially, you will find much to explore.

To complete the South Hams part of the Coast Path, you will leave Dartmouth on the ferry to Kingswear, where you will find a private railway boasting steam locomotives running between here and Paignton. The path heads out towards the woods, offering excellent views across the estuary. The Daymark, built to help Royal Mail ships find the harbour entrance in the nineteenth century is passed, and you come to the area part managed and part owned by the National Trust, offering varied features of interest, from wildlife to the beautiful gardens of Coleton Fishacre. On to Scabbacombe, the beach with its waterfall offering the promise of a swim, and the end of the South Hams stretch of the Path is near. Down to Man sands, and up again to the cliff top, remarkable for its complex geology, where Sharkham Point offers splendid views, behind to remind you of the remoter places you have walked, and ahead to the bustling port of Brixham. It is perhaps fitting that the urban centres of Paignton and Torbay adjoin the Path at this point, just as Plymouth adjoins it at the western end. The contrast with the small historic villages and open ruggedness of the South Hams coast could hardly be clearer.

Whether you walk in summer or winter, as a serious expedition or for a gentle stroll, may the Coastal Path give you pleasure. You are certain to find that once you have begun to make its acquaintance, you will wish to know it better.